R. West

D1607763

Montale,
Debussy, and Modernism

# Princeton Essays on the Arts

For a complete list
of books in this series,
see page 159.

# Montale,
# Debussy, and Modernism

Gian-Paolo Biasin

Princeton University Press

Princeton, New Jersey

Library of Congress Cataloging-in-Publication Data

Biasin, Gian-Paolo.
    Montale, Debussy, and modernism.
    (Princeton essays on the arts)
    Translation of: Il vento di Debussy.
    Bibliography: p.
    Includes index.
    1. Montale, Eugenio, 1896–1981—Criticism and
interpretation. 2. Debussy, Claude, 1862–1918—
Influence. 3. Ut pictura poesis (Aesthetics)
4. Europe—Intellectual life—20th century. I. Title.
II. Series.
PQ4829.0565Z568613 1989      851'.12      89-10516
ISBN 0-691-06790-2
ISBN 0-691-01466-3 (pbk.)

# Contents

# Illustrations

# Preface

Eugenio Montale's poetry is such that it causes not only long-lasting fidelities but also broad resonances, reverberations, and comparisons which expand it and involve it in the European culture of the twentieth century in a subtle, often elusive, yet pervasive manner. In this book I want to explore some of these resonances, part of these reverberations, two such comparisons. I want to keep Montale's poetry at the center of my discourse and at the same time go around it by little-known paths which may be winding, rich with ramifications, intersections, and invitations.

In my itinerary I discuss the possible homologies between poetry and music, not in the well-known area of the relationship between libretto and score in opera, but in the more particular one of the formal and thematic choices which marked a modern turning point in both music and poetry. In this area, although I am not a musicologist, I try to show the importance of Claude Debussy not only, as is obvious, for the musical innovations of our century (all the way to Arnold Schönberg and dodecaphony), but for poetry as well, and for the young Montale in particular. In Debussy the wind is a theme, a musical image, a literary topos which, while hearkening back to romanticism, opens up unexpected passages in our understanding of twentieth-century poetry; it is an invaluable and indispensable prelude, with its sweeping presence over a land or a sea-scape, to the appearance on the scene of the modern artist, usually presented as an antihero (or clown, or mounte-bank). The young Montale was fascinated by modern art in all of its forms: Debussy and music, as well as the im-pressionist and postimpressionist painters, the English verse-narrators, and the great fiction writers of our cen-tury, *in primis*, Italo Svevo.

In my second itinerary I search for the possible homol-ogies between poetry and painting in a specific area which does not include influences on or preferences by the young Montale, but is concerned with objective (that is, formal, thematic, and ideological) comparisons between his early poems and the work of the great Italian painter and engraver, Giorgio Morandi, whom he did not even know at that time. I also try to reinterpret the Horatian topos of "ut pictura poesis" in light of contemporary criti-cal theories but with accurate attention to the formal val-ues of the pictorial and poetic texts I examine. Even in this case I must face a field which is not mine, art criticism; I have entered it with great respect, and I derive from it the joy of a greater understanding not only of painting, but of literature as well.

I return to literature alone in the last itinerary, by ex-ploring the difficult relationship between (lyric) poetry and (novelistic) prose in the twentieth century. While ac-knowledging—as Cesare Segre did recently—that the two genres are intrinsically different, I have tried to under-score their homologies, which do exist and are made even more important, in my view, by what Mikhail Bakhtin called "the novelization of literature." In this context, the presence of the antihero (clown, Schlemihl) in the novels of Italo Svevo and Luigi Pirandello as well as in Montale's poetry becomes a fundamental interpretive key of modern art.

The epilogue is intended to pull together the threads of the interdisciplinary discourse developed in the three essays of the volume; it is intended to be the final intersection where the paths I follow converge—at least temporarily, because an intersection is always open to further roads.

Both the interdisciplinary approach and the emphasis on the theme of the clown suggest the critical proposal at the core of the entire work: the (belated) acknowledgment of modernism as a fundamental component of Italian culture. This acknowledgment, it seems to me, is indispensable in order to align at last twentieth-century Italian culture with its Anglo-Saxon and French counterparts. The latter two have been even too hegemonic so far, while the former actually deserves to be recognized in its best voices and achievements.

The complexity of the subject matter made me provide the text with an apparatus of both broad and specific footnotes which account for the sources I used and suggest further probes into single problems. In this context, I have also given brief bio-bibliographical sketches of a few critics important in Italy but not necessarily familiar to the American reader (for example, Vittorio Pica, Roberto Longhi, Francesco Arcangeli, or Ezio Raimondi).

The essays that make up this book originally appeared in different and even preliminary versions in various publications: the first in *La Regione Liguria* 10 (1982), n. 12, in *Rassegna di Studi Italiani* 1 (1983), n. 2, and in *La poesia di Eugenio Montale: Atti del convegno internazionale, Genova, Novembre 1982*, ed. Sergio Campailla and Cesare Federico Goffis (Florence: Le Monnier, 1984); the second in *Intersezioni* 2 (1982), n. 1; and part of the third in *Italian Literature: Roots and Branches*, ed. Giose Rimanelli and K. J. Atchity (New Haven: Yale University Press, 1976). My thanks to the respective editors and publishers. These essays were collected and molded into the Italian edition of this book, *Il vento di Debussy: La poesia di Montale nella cultura del Novecento* (Bologna: Il Mulino, 1985).

In my translation I have followed the Italian text closely, only adding a few clarifications where I thought they were needed, according to the valuable suggestions of a reader. I provide the texts of Montale's poems first in the original, immediately followed by my literal rendering in English, which seems preferable to more elegant translations already available in print, because my textual analyses are necessarily based on the Italian, especially at the phonic level. Permission to quote the Italian texts of Montale's poetry (© Arnoldo Mondadori Editore, 1948-77) as well as my own translations is kindly granted by New Directions Publishing Corporation, © 1965-80 for *Selected Poems, New Poems*, and *It Depends: A Poet's Notebook*.

I wish to thank my students of the seminars in which I discussed and commented on Montale, my friends who read the manuscript, the readers of Princeton University Press, and Julie Marvin, the manuscript editor, for their valuable comments and suggestions. I dedicate this book to E. R., who on the paths of Tilden Park pointed out to me those other paths, of culture and friendship. I also wish to dedicate the present edition to Glauco Cambon, *in memoriam*: his "inclusive flame," his passion for poetry (and notably Montale's) still shines for me and for all the other readers of modern art.

Montale,
Debussy, and Modernism

# 1 | Debussy and the Wind

J'aime à la fureur
les choses où le son se mêle à la lumière.
CHARLES BAUDELAIRE, *Les bijoux*

## Poetry and Music

Eugenio Montale makes a decisive assertion in the "Imaginary Interview" of 1946, from which it is appropriate to begin:

> When I started writing the first poems of *Ossi di seppia* [Cuttlefish bones] I certainly had an idea of the new music and the new painting. I had heard Debussy's "Minstrels," and in the first edition of my book there was a little thing that tried to remake it, "Musica sognata" [Dreamed music]. And I had looked at *Gl'impressionisti* by the too defamed Vittorio Pica.[1]

Even in its typically Montalean caution ("I had an idea," "I had looked at"), this a posteriori assertion of an intention and an awareness fundamental to the beginning of an entire poetic oeuvre maintains a basic importance, an importance enhanced by the recent reappearance in the critical edition of precisely that "little thing" mentioned here. In fact, the statement is a proud vindication of cultural openness and novelty ("the new music, the new painting"—the

3

repetition of the adjective is not casual, but rhetorically re-
vealing). Montale's words are to be taken as a valuable
piece of information and not as a misleading indication for
the critic tracking the origins of Montale's poetry and the
cultural framework in which it belonged and succeeded.

To start with, there appear in the opening quotation
Montale's three basic lifelong interests: poetry, music, and
painting. It is not really necessary to recall the elements,
the occasions, the biographical anecdotes in which these
interests were articulated and variously expressed—from
his pastels with delightful seascapes and smiling portraits
to his studies to become a professional baritone, studies
which Montale soon abandoned but never forgot, and
transferred later to his punctilious activity as a demanding
and even idiosyncratic music critic for the leading Mil-
anese daily *Il corriere della sera*.[2] Rather, the interaction
among poetry, music, and painting points out for the con-
temporary critic the complexity of culture, as it is theo-
rized specifically in Bakhtin's dialogic principle, a com-
plexity Montale had understood and noted clearly on his
own, with great effectiveness.[3] In fact, the interaction
among different genres, expressive modes, languages, and
codes by itself is not sufficient: it must be an active and
innovative interaction, which should experiment with new
possibilities and seek new horizons, by translating the re-
sults in one field into another and by transferring one lan-
guage into another. And that is exactly what Montale did.

It is first necessary to ask why Montale points out the
new music, particularly Debussy, and the new painting,
particularly the impressionists. Certainly, these expressive
forms have been congenial to poetry in a centuries-old tra-
dition, from "ut pictura poesis" all the way to "de la mu-
sique avant toute chose." They are especially congenial to
the young Montale, given the biographical data just men-
tioned.[4]

But why the impressionists, and why Debussy?

Briefly we can say, echoing Félix Fénéon, that the impressionists were among the first to lay the foundations of modern painting, through the separation and matching of pure colors on the surface of the painting. The viewer had to mix and fuse these colors together by active perception, thus recreating that visual harmony—and hence the object itself of the painter's vision—which might have seemed lost at first impression: one thinks of Monet's Rouen Cathedral, St. Lazare Station, and haystacks, or of Seurat's Grande Jatte, with their elaborate variations of light and the "infinite delicacy of the modelling."[5] It is therefore *style*, with its disjunction between sign and meaning, which the impressionists emphasize at the expense of representation and objectivity; and it is the active participation of the viewer's eye they require as an integral part of the artistic process—perhaps because, as Walter Benjamin has suggested, the experience of the urban crowd was a new spectacle to which the eye had to become accustomed, thus acquiring a new capacity for vision, of which the impressionist technique would be but a reflection.[6]

Analogously, Debussy was among the very first to unhinge the traditional tonal system, with deliberate dissonances which broke the harmonic scale and had to be received and accepted by the ears of the listener, who was thereby oriented toward the intrinsic and autonomous musicality of the single sounds. In the new poetry, lexical dissonance and analogic words are the two critical categories that, after Friedrich, vigorously characterize the modern developments and their relationships with music and painting.

I do not know whether Montale had such relationships and analogies clearly in mind from the beginning, with all their complexity and ramifications. Probably he did not. But he had certainly understood the importance of the book by Pica, the Neapolitan art critic who had indeed been "too defamed," if one remembers that Ardengo Soffici called him "an imbecile," while Fénéon, in contrast, had stressed his "rare coherence" and mental openness without biases or dogmatism.[7] To be sure, *Gl'impressionisti* presents a remarkable overview of the impressionist movement, from its English precursors to the late followers of Italian divisionism (Giovanni Segantini, Angelo Morbelli, Gaetano Previati, Giuseppe Pellizza da Volpedo, and others); above all, Pica's book contains an idea derived from Fénéon and still fundamental today for the understanding of the impressionists, that is, "their use of spots of pure colors which become fused at a distance on the pupil of the beholder" rather than on the palette of the painter.[8]

But the very fact that Montale cites the impressionists and Debussy together seems to indicate that he considered pictorial and musical impressionism on the same plane, while as far as Debussy is concerned, such a label, even if current then, has been critically reviewed and is no longer considered valid today. It is important to note, as Laura Barile did, that "attention to what was happening in the musical world is characteristic of the culture" of the early twentieth century: for example, "also [Renato] Serra was exploring the same area of the musicality of verse, a musicality intended in quantitative terms, arsis and thesis, rhythm and no longer melody." In such a context it seems useful to recall *La dissonanza*, the musical journal edited by Giannotto Bastianelli and Ildebrando Pizzetti, with its emblematically programmatic title pointing to the new music.[9]

In any case, whether or not Montale was aware of all the implications of the relationship among the expressive novelties in the three arts is not really important. What matters, and it matters greatly, is that he lived this relationship from the very beginning with extraordinary sensitivity and timeliness; that all his early poetry was enriched by this relationship or interaction; and in particular (leaving painting aside for the moment), that he never disavowed his original preference for Debussy, but repeatedly and skillfully used it for his aims of poetic and cultural politics, in ways and contexts that are worth exploring.

Montale's discourse on Debussy is fragmentary, seemingly occasional and discontinuous, but actually intimately coherent and rigorous when its pieces are put together. Montale's remarks are theoretical, historical, and cultural. At the theoretical level, the relationship of music and poetry is acknowledged by Montale throughout musical aesthetics, from madrigals to opera librettos. The vexed question of the superiority of one over the other is solved in the sense that "poetry and music progress each on its own, and their encounter remains dependent on occasional chances" (as in the cases of Debussy, Mussorgsky, and Schönberg), because, says Montale, following Mallarmé, "poetry is itself already music." He repeated this idea in 1962: "I know that the art of the word is itself music, even if it has little to do with the laws of acoustics."[10]

It might be objected that such a proud assertion of the poetic word's self-sufficiency is contradicted by the initial statement implied in the effort of remaking "Minstrels": it is true, but only on the surface, because precisely by remaking Debussy Montale reasserts the superiority of the word over music, whose "asemantic" character, "a great acquisition of modern culture,"[11] is thus thematized, conceptualized, by the only form of art capable of carrying out such an operation explicitly, that is, the written word, and in particular the poetic word. This is so true that in the same imaginary interview Montale mentions the great contemporary "isms" prevalent in European philosophy: "Marforio's big words": Lev Šcestov's Kierkegaardian existentialism, Giovanni Gentile's absolute immanentism, Benedetto Croce's "idealistic positivism," and above all, for the years of *Ossi di seppia*, Étienne Boutroux's contingentism. He does so in order to deny all of them immediately afterwards—but the mentioning itself, which is "semantic," remains:

> No, in writing my first book (a book that got written by itself) I did not rely on such ideas. . . . I obeyed a need

of musical expression. I wanted my word to be more adherent than those of other poets I had known. More adherent to what? It seemed to me I was living under a glass bell, yet I felt I was close to something essential. A thin veil, just a thread separated me from the definitive quid. The absolute experience would have been the tearing of that veil, of that thread: an explosion, the end of the deceit of the world as representation. But this was an unreachable limit. And my will to adhere remained musical, instinctive, not programmatic. I wanted to twist the neck of the eloquence of our old aulic language, even at the cost of a counter-eloquence.[12]

No "isms," then. But in light of poetry's autonomy and of its semantic character, this need for a musical expression says quite a lot about Montale's faith in the written word, from the very beginning. Perhaps it might be appropriate to try to point out possible functional and structural homologies between music and poetry, as Leonard Bernstein has done recently in Chomskyan terms, with impassionate remarks in which the transformations of generative grammar (at the phonologic, symbolic, and semantic level) are convincingly applied to the "reading" of great texts of Western music.[13] But Montale's skepticism on the point remains, and the literary critic must acknowledge it and recognize first the fact that the poet's major efforts to link poetry and music in some way belong entirely to his very early period, and include only a few poems never collected in a volume, that is, never elevated to the dignity of the oeuvre in verse: "Musica silenziosa" (Silent music), "Suonatina di pianoforte" (Piano sonatina), "Accordi" (Accords), and the first section of *Ossi*, titled "Movimenti," musical movements à la Debussy ("Mouvements" is one of the *Images* for piano). The movements are, however, already metaphoric: "Ascoltami, i poeti laureati / *si muovono . . .*" (Listen to me, the poets laureate / *move . . .*). In the definitive edition, they include "I limoni" (The lemon trees), "Corno inglese" (English horn), "Falsetto," and "Minstrels," while the suite "Mediterraneo" (Mediterranean Sea) indeed owes to Debussy's *La mer*, as Marzio Pieri noted, but I would say more as an idea than as a performance.[14]

In subsequent developments of Montale's poetry there will be only echoes or calculated musical references without any systematic intention, as, to give just two examples, in the motet "Infuria sale o grandine" (Salt or hail rages), which hearkens back to Debussy's "La cathédrale engloutie" ("very likely"[15]), or in "La bufera" (The storm) with its memory of "Jardins sous la pluie," again by Debussy.

Meanwhile, however, at the historical level, Montale knows well that music, painting, and poetry follow their parallel paths, which may or may not coincide in time and correspond in space. Let us consider along with him "some dates" concerning decadentism:

> The pre-Raphaelites were active in England when in Italy the like of [Antonio] Fontanesi and [Michele] Cammarano were painting, who were classical notwithstanding their romanticism. Rimbaud and Mallarmé write at a time when in Italy the "scapigliati" group is barely born; our "macchiaioli" painters wake up when they encounter French impressionism; Debussy is a contemporary of Puccini and Mascagni. D'Annunzio cannot be explained without his foreign sources, which are innumerable. While in Vienna expressionism rages, in Italy [Alfredo] Casella and company propound a return to the eighteenth century.[16]

Let us agree that "luckily in Italy we are late," as Montale asserts in concluding his survey with a smiling but salutary historiographic irony. However, in doing so Montale has dotted his i's and given us the basic data to understand his cultural operation, in which Debussy—a true litmus paper—plays a central function. Let us follow Montale's discourse in the literary field:

> [Guido Gozzano] reduced D'Annunzio just as Debussy had scaled down Wagner, but without ever achieving results that could be termed Debussyan. Gozzano's poetry remains in that climate that scholars of the late nineteenth-century Italian melodrama called "verista"—a climate which ultimately is not of decadent origin. . . . It seems certain to me that in Gozzano the romantic-bourgeois "verista" element was the most fruitful one. Gozzano reduced the Italian poetry of his time to a lowest common denominator, and here the comparison with Puccini is again irresistible.[17]

Actually, against the reductive arguments of some contemporary detractors, "try to erase Puccini and Gozzano from the framework of their time and tell me if an unfillable void would not be created."[18] But, once the historical judgment and the value judgment are established, we should note the impeccable exactness of Montale's reasoning, in which the musical references are in a dialogic relationship with the literary data. In such a context, we know that Puccini was, polemically for Montale, "late" in comparison with Debussy, and that if we use a qualitative criterion Gozzano cannot be considered a wholly successful innovator ("without ever achieving results that could be termed Debussyan").[19] And if Montale gives Gozzano his due ("he was the first who made sparks by making the aulic clash with the prosaic"), nevertheless Montale also reminds us of his own Verlainean intention "to twist the neck of the eloquence of our old aulic language, even at the risk of a counter-eloquence." Therefore, although Debussy is at the center of the argument, the true target is actually D'Annunzio. Just as in modern music Debussy reduced and hence in a sense replaced Wagner, so in Italian literature D'Annunzio would be reduced and superseded not by Gozzano, but by Montale—the same Montale who "passed through" D'Annunzio. After all, music was added to D'Annunzio (in *Le martyre de Saint Sébastien*) by Debussy, who in turn was "set to poetry" precisely by Montale![20]

## 2. Claude Debussy

It is appropriate to devote some further attention to Debussy, and try to understand better (or more explicitly, in a more detailed manner) than Montale did the novelty and the importance of his work both in the development of contemporary music and in its relation to literature. We have to consider a cultural context of which music is part as a signifying system "where particular relationships occur between signifier and signified, and in its own way this system symbolizes the great themes of culture: the relationships with the Other, with nature, with death, with desire."[21]

In musical historiography, Debussy holds a very singular position. The Italian musicologist Guido Salvetti characterizes him as a "participant in the intellectual and moral engagement of the Wagnerian-decadent composers, inclined toward a 'light' art, made of innuendoes and analogies; an indefatigable searcher (who renewed himself till his death) for a musical language that should express both the spiritual evanescence of inner experiences and the formal rigor of a conscious and perfectly responsible artistic operation."[22]

I have chosen these words by Salvetti because they seem to me very effective in outlining the historical-substantial and critical-formal elements of Debussy's work. Another Italian musicologist, Mario Bortolotto, echoes these words when he states that Debussy's aversion "to any form of *naturalisme* . . . pushed him inexorably toward imprecision, vagueness, even the mystery construed by questionable writers" with symbolist tastes; Debussy had some inclinations toward "yet undetermined pulsions," which, however, had to find "their configuration, and actually their identity, in the rigor of form."[23] For his part, Pierre Boulez insists that Debussy remains isolated in the musical history of the West, because with him "the unstable, the instant burst into music," and above all "a relative and irreversible conception of musical time, and more generally of the universe of music" was born: "In the organization of sounds, this conception is translated above all into a refusal of the existing harmonic hierarchies as the sole data of the world of sounds."[24] Even more generally, this conception opens the doors to modern music, which, like the novel according to Bakhtin, is characterized by heteroglossia, or linguistic plurality, in that no musical language has succeeded in assuming a dominant position.[25]

But in the meantime it is worth quoting a statement made by Debussy to his teacher, Ernest Guiraud, back in 1889: "I am not tempted to imitate what I admire in Wagner. I conceive a different dramatic form: music begins where the word is impotent to express: music is written for the inexpressible. I would like that music seemed to emerge from the shade, and after a few instants re-entered it. . . . I dream of poems that do not condemn me to drag long, heavy acts, . . . poems where the characters do not discuss but suffer life and destiny." Bortolotto comments that "it is an impeccable assertion, for its clarity and intensity, of an anxiety to represent" which "already goes beyond the pillars of symbolism."[26] In any case, such intentions of the early Debussy are carried out in his major works, from *Prélude à l'après-midi d'un faune* (1894) to *Nocturnes* (1900) and *Pelléas et Mélisande* (1902). These works make up what was called, because of not entirely justified analogies, Debussy's musical "impressionism." He was not actually an impressionist, "although he provided some pretexts for such a limitation: the misunderstanding derives from the titles [of some compositions], and from the fact that his character, Monsieur Croche, 'spoke of an orchestral score as if it were a painting': a simple question of an antidilettante."[27]

Actually, in his revolutionary novelty, Debussy tended toward "the dissolution of the solidity, the grandiosity, the compactness of the musical language of the late German romanticism."[28] Wagner had exacerbated the tension in the traditional harmonic system whereby each accord tends toward another.[29] In contrast, Debussy wanted to "break up this tension, which is often artificial, and regain the sound value of each single accord taken by itself," in various ways: by putting "dissonant accords next to one another," by passing "from a consonant accord to another belonging to a different tonality," and through "the lesser force of appeal of the 'point of repose,' that is, of the tonal center" (for example, through the pentatonic scale or defective scales); the consequent "slackening of the harmonic tension" produces ever purer sounds.[30]

Debussy carried out an analogous operation on the traditional rhythmic setup, through long pauses, suspensions, repetitions, and variations; coherently in his orchestration he dissolved the orchestral mass of the German symphonic system and preferred pure timbres and soloist instruments, "above all flute, oboe, and English horn."[31] As a further commentary I shall quote a passage from the analysis of *Prélude à l'après-midi d'un faune* in which Bernstein emphasizes that the *Prélude* is "a masterpiece of structure, . . . carefully composed, intentionally designed" on the tritone, "the absolute negation of tonality"—not only that, but the harmonic implications of the tritone ("the whole-tone scale, a unique invention of Debussy's") produce "the first organized atonal material ever to appear in musical history." Bernstein's conclusion is lapidary; the *Prélude* "is actually an essay on E major."[32]

In both his orchestral and—especially—piano works after 1902, Debussy emphasizes "the new rigor linking harmony and melody," and, "instead of concealing the melodic and rhythmic line in an impressionistic halo, evidences it neatly" (back in 1910-11, Jacques Rivière had remarked that Debussy's was "a music of delight," but also "exact, rigorous, rarefied by intelligence," and "touching because of its very rigor").[33]

The innovation of sound thought is achieved through the irony of pieces like "Golliwogg's Cakewalk" or "The Little Shepherd," is remarkable in *Images* of 1905-1907 and in the twenty-four piano *Préludes* of 1910-1913, and is definitive in the last works, particularly in the twelve piano *Études* of 1915, where, "following the stimulation of mechanical-technical developments, there occurs a total emancipation of dissonance, and the topoi of twentieth-century piano music are explored."[34]

Summing up, it is possible to agree with Jarocinski, who states that Debussy's aesthetics corresponds fundamentally to Mallarmé's poetics: "Both of them are poles apart from Wagner; they searched for 'the essence of things,' the bare truths, not deformed by flat spatial categories or by a pompous rhetoric."[35] In fact, Boulez's lapidary judgment should be quoted here: "We cannot forget that the time of Debussy is also the time of Cézanne and Mallarmé: a triple conjunction which is, perhaps, at the root of every modernity."[36]

I hope that the brief preceding remarks, besides defining Debussy's place in the music of his time, clearly indicate his importance in the dialogic relations with literature. Here I take a completely opposite approach from Arthur Wenk's analysis, which shows the influence of some poets (especially Banville, Baudelaire, Verlaine, Louÿs, and Mallarmé) on Debussy's musical choices and solutions. On the contrary, I wish to characterize the influence of Debussy's music on Montale's early poems, following the indication of the poet.

Debussy's influence is first of all, and not too paradoxically, a literary one, because for Montale "Debussy, as a musician, was a great *homme de lettres*, a very open mind that could have expressed itself even outside music, and this is a measure of his importance."[37] Hence we can say that the very literate musician filtered and handed down the great lesson of French symbolism to which Montale hearkens back (like Giuseppe Ungaretti, but in a different manner), with great awareness of his own debts as well as of his own autonomy.[38] This is so true that Montale poses "the Browning-Baudelaire junction" (not Mallarmé) at the origins of "all modern poetry."[39] He also states that, "starting from Baudelaire and part of Browning, and sometimes from their confluence," a current of poetry was developed, "not realistic, not romantic and not even strictly decadent, which *grosso modo* can be termed metaphysical. I was born in that wake." To make things absolutely clear, Montale finally adds, "Be it understood that I do not care much about the label 'metaphysical,' because the area of this type of poetry is extremely uncertain. All the art that does not give up reason, but is born of the clash of reason with something that is not reason, might be called metaphysical."[40]

A second influence of Debussy is to be emphasized in the antigrandiosity of Montale's style and in the antiheroism of his characters who do not discuss but suffer: certainly they are cultural models to be found not only in Maurice Maeterlink's theatre but in so much literature of the twentieth century. This influence can be documented, as far as Montale is concerned, in his poetics of *diminutio antiaulica* in "I limoni," and in his antihero par excellence, Arsenio, who is foreshadowed by "Minstrels," among other poems. We should also stress Debussy's "emancipation of dissonance," which was later taken up and theorized by Igor Stravinsky in his *Poétique musicale* of 1942, significantly quoted at the beginning of Friedrich's book in order to characterize modern poetry and its structure.[41] Through lexical dissonance, modern poets want to express an even deeper, inner dissonance, and there is no doubt that Montale is an absolutely central and genuine voice in this kind of lyric and modern poetry. Also, a precise although not lasting influence by Debussy can be noticed in the early poems by Montale: three out of the seven "Accordi" bear the names of three of Debussy's favorite instruments in orchestration: flute, oboe, and English horn (and it should be noted that another poem of the same period, "Suonatina di pianoforte," perhaps precisely because it is written "alla Maurizio Ravel" and not à la Claude Debussy, remains in the limbo of uncollected works).[42]

Finally, not so much an influence as a consonance or a profound correspondence is to be emphasized at the thematic level: the sea plays a very remarkable role in Debussy's music as well as in the poetry of the Ligurian Montale; often accompanied by the wind, a sonorous element which completes its figurative character, the sea is present in numerous compositions by the two artists as a source of inspiration, an interlocutor, and a descriptive, narrative or discursive pretext. A particular comment by Jarocinski is worth quoting:

> Monet's seascapes are never terrifying. We take part in the contemplation of the painter who is in a pantheistic accord with nature. But in Debussy's *La mer* everything seems to occur—as in Turner—at a cosmic level. In the final part of this polyrhythmic symphony, "Le dialogue du vent et de la mer," the woeful sound of the storm seems to announce death and destruction. The same impression emanates from the seventh prelude of book one, "Ce qu'a vu le vent de l'Ouest."[43]

It seems unnecessary to underscore how pertinent these remarks are to Montale's poetry as well, from "Arsenio" to "La bufera." But it is time now to verify the aspects of Debussy's influence on and consonance with Montale's texts.

## 3. "Minstrels" and "Corno inglese"

I shall not devote a systematic analysis to "Accordi" and the other "musical" poems of the young Montale, but I will remark on some aspects of these poems that seem important; these remarks should be added to what critics like

Marco Forti, Edoardo Sanguineti and Silvio Ramat have already pointed out.[44] A valuable testimony of a cultural season characterized by extraordinary intensity and fervor, the suite of seven "Accordi" allows us to verify textually the incidence on Montale's poetry of contemporary Italian movements (Dannunzianism and "crepuscolarismo," already noted by critics), as well as of preceding and foreign ones: in particular, impressionism and symbolism. Impressionism is traceable in verses like

> e a questa ciarla
> s'univano altre, ma più gravi, e come
> bolle di vetro luminose intorno
> stellavano la notte che raggiava.
> Di contro al cielo buio erano sagome
> di perle,
> grandi flore di fuochi d'artifizio,
> cupole di cristallo . . . .

> and to this chat
> others were united, but more serious ones, and like
> luminous glass bubbles around
> they starred the radiating night.
> Against the dark sky there were outlines
> of pearls,
> great floras of fireworks,
> crystal domes . . . .

These lines from "Flauti-Fagotti" (Flutes-bassoons) also display the analogic word and the alliteration of "grandi flore di fuochi d'artifizio." Symbolism is traceable not only in the typical use of capital letters in key words like "il Centro" (the Center) and "il Niente" (the Nothingness) in "Violoncelli" (Cellos), or "il Brutto" (the Ugly) in "Contrabbasso" (Contrabass), but also in the numerous cases of analogic words: for example, "Occhi corolle s'aprono / in me—chissà?—o nel suolo" (Eyes corollas open up / in me—who knows?—or on the ground), with its chiasmatic structure in "Violini" (Violins), or the song that goes "nelle vene" (into the veins) and then "nel cuore" (into the heart) in "Violoncelli." Symbolism is also present in lexical dissonances such as the beautiful oxymoron of "Flauti-Fagotti": "gli occhi s'abbacinavano / in un gaio supplizio!" (the eyes were blinded / in a gay torment).[45]

The "Accordi" suite is a true orchestral rehearsal of themes and motives that will be found again throughout Montale's poetic oeuvre, from the expectation of a miracle to the greyness of daily life, from sadness to a fragile joy or rare happiness, from perplexity or existential bewilderment to the invention of the female interlocutor "tu"(you). But let us take up "Minstrels," the only poem derived explicitly "da C. Debussy," as the epigraph states, published under the title "Musica sognata" (Dreamed music) in the first edition of *Ossi di seppia,* then omitted because too explicit, and finally reinserted with its Debussyan title in the definitive edition.[46]

Montale had heard Debussy's "Minstrels" in March, 1917. There is a detailed and revealing testimony of it in the poet's diary, recently published by Laura Barile with loving care:

> Concert. Last night concert at the Carlo Felice Theatre. André Hekking cellist and Luigi La Volpe pianist. I was there with Bonzi. Beautiful. Here is a resume. . . . Debussy, "Les collines d'Anacapri" and "Ménestrels": descriptive and impressionistic music, filled with disconnectedness, colors, and meters. First it leaves you almost indifferent, if not hostile; but then it remains imprinted, as if in a nightmare; and you would like to hear it over and over. "Les collines" ends with a white key, dissonant and jarring like the cry of a lost bird. "Ménestrels" is, or is taken to be, ironic music. Excellent performance. Why didn't I study music too? I have been asking myself for a long time. Who knows whether pure music wouldn't be my life! How

many ideas flash in my mind, which might mislead the public![47]

This diary entry, so sharp and impassionate, clearly shows the impact the encounter with Debussy's new music had on the young Montale. This music, although defined as "descriptive and impressionistic" (according to the criteria prevalent at the time) strikes the poet for its dissonance and irony, and above all "remains imprinted as if in a nightmare": so that it can be said that it is the occasion-spur for the poem under examination—and by the way, the transformation of music into poetry is already present in the diary entry, in the beautiful simile of "a white key, dissonant and jarring like the cry of a lost bird."

Let us listen then, first of all, to the musical text from which the poetic one was derived: it is the twelfth of the piano *Préludes*, and we might listen to the performance by Walter Gieseking, "the candid Gieseking" as Massimo Mila calls him.[48] From a formal viewpoint, this piece is remarkable because it illustrates in specific terms my general presentation of Debussy: in it "the sequels of accords have no functional character. A quick design creates associations of sounds, and it would be useless to find a justification for this in the norms of traditional harmony."[49] It is the novelty of the rhythm that imposes itself, a bit as in "Golliwogg's Cakewalk." But perhaps, for the literary critic interested in the dialogic relationships of culture, the thematic aspects of this prelude are even more important than the formal ones.

"Minstrels" is not the only piece by Debussy dealing with the same topic. It should be remembered that he set poems by Banville ("Pierrot") and Verlaine ("Fêtes galantes"), in which, via Watteau, there are characters from the Italian commedia dell'arte: Colombine, Pierrot, and Harlequin, some of whom will reappear, together with Doctor Balanzone, in Debussy's ballet *Masques et Bergamasques* composed for Diaghilev in 1909.[50] We can in fact speak of a true musical topos in this connection: Stravinsky's *Petroushka* appeared in 1911, Schönberg's *Pierrot lunaire* in 1912, and Stravinsky's *Pulcinella* in 1920.[51] Even in contemporary iconography the mask, the clown, the minstrel, the mountebank become the protagonists of an entire pictorial story which links theatrical and musical motives, as can be seen in these few interconnected examples: Paul Cézanne's "Harlequin" (1888-1890), Pablo Picasso's "Harlequin and His Family" (1905), Georges Braque's "Man with Guitar" (1911), Picasso's "Harlequin with Violin" (1918), Gino Severini's sketch for Stravinsky's ballet *Pulcinella* (1920), and again Severini's and Picasso's "Masks" (1922 and 1921 respectively). Analogously, for the corresponding literary topos, we might first recall the figure of the philosopher-dancer in Nietzsche's *Thus Spoke Zarathustra*, but in any case Italian examples should suffice: Gian Pietro Lucini's "L'intermezzo dell'Arlecchinata" (1898), Corrado Govoni's "Le poesie d'Arlecchino" (1907), Ardengo Soffici's "Arlecchino" (1914), the Chaplinesque gestures of Italo Svevo's Zeno or the dissociations of Luigi Pirandello's *Naked Masks*, and above all the attitudes of the "crepuscolari" poets, culminating perhaps in the emblematic lines by Aldo Palazzeschi of 1909:

Chi sono?
Il saltimbanco dell'anima mia.

Who am I?
The mountebank of my soul.

It is indeed a fascinating topos, which became the subject of an elegant and by now classic book by Jean Starobinski appropriately titled *Portrait de l'artiste en saltimbanque*.[52] One of the reasons why this topos is so fascinating is that it is an expression (common to all forms of art) of what we might call the antiheroism of modern culture, to which we shall pay close attention in chapter 3. For the moment,

against this background, we can now read Montale's own
version of "Minstrels":

Ritornello, rimbalzi
tra le vetrate d'afa dell'estate.

Acre groppo di note soffocate,
riso che non esplode
ma trapunge le ore vuote
e lo suonano tre avanzi di baccanale
vestiti di ritagli di giornali,
con istrumenti mai veduti,
simili a strani imbuti
che si gonfiano a volte e poi s'afflosciano.

Musica senza rumore
che nasce dalle strade,
s'innalza a stento e ricade,
e si colora di tinte
ora scarlatte ora biade,
e inumidisce gli occhi, così che il mondo
si vede come socchiudendo gli occhi
nuotar nel biondo.

Scatta ripiomba sfuma,
poi riappare
soffocata e lontana: si consuma.
Non s'ode quasi, si respira.
                    Bruci
tu pure tra le lastre dell'estate,
cuore che ti smarrisci! Ed ora incauto
provi le ignote note sul tuo flauto.

Refrain, you bounce
among the summer sultriness' glass windows.

Harsh knot of strangled notes,
laughter which does not explode
but embroiders the empty hours
and three dregs of a revelry play it,

dressed with newspaper clips,
with instruments never seen before
similar to strange funnels
which swell at times and then become flabby.

Music without noise
which is born from the streets,
hardly rises and falls back,
and is colored with dyes
now scarlet now faded,
and moistens the eyes, so that the world
is seen as if half-closing the eyes
swimming in the blond.

It spurts plunges fades,
then it reappears
strangled and afar: it is consumed.
It is not heard, almost, it is breathed.
  You burn
too, among the slabs of summer,
heart that gets lost! And now unwary
you try the unknown notes on your flute.

Montale adheres to Debussy's text first of all themati-
cally: the subject of his poem is the music played by the
minstrels of the title, or more specifically the strolling mu-
sicians suggested by the English noun, who become the
"three dregs of a revelry" (or "paradoxical men" according
to another version of the text), "dressed in newspaper
clips" in the poet's very modern interpretation. Indeed
they seem "snatched from some futurist collage," and cer-
tainly they are the "figurative correlatives," midway be-
tween fauvism and cubism, of the "primarily phonic and
rhythmic essence" of this brief poem.[53]
  It is to be noted that the kind of music in "Minstrels" is,
specifically, a refrain, that is, a repetition-variation which
is typically musical and is achieved accordingly by Montale
with the second and the penultimate line ("tra le vetrate

d'afa dell'estate"—"tu pure tra le lastre dell'estate") and with the comparison between the refrain itself and the heart, both of which burn in the summer heat. Finally, the musical subject is the very form of the poem, with its rhythm, now spurting, now nuanced, with the harsh sounds of its phonic texture (for instance "acre groppo di note soffocate"), and with the small dissonances of imperfect rhymes, such as rimbalzi—avanzi, esplode—vuote, and baccanale—giornali.

With this "little thing" that tries to remake Debussy, Montale pays his cultural debt and leaves a precise indication about it for his readers. But this indication can be misleading, not because of what it says, but because of what it hides. In fact, the poem has a typically Montalean, poetic and metapoetic element, that "heart" which is here still uncertain (it gets lost like the heart of "Corno inglese," a "scordato strumento," a forgotten/untuned instrument), but already burns in the summer heat. This burning is nothing more than a hint here, but is very important because it will be developed later at crucial moments of *Ossi di seppia*. From "Non rifugiarti nell'ombra" (Don't take refuge in the shade):

> tali i nostri animi arsi
> in cui l'illusione brucia
> un fuoco pieno di cenere. . . .

> such are our dry souls
> in which illusion burns
> a fire full of ash. . . .

From "Ciò che di me sapeste" (What you knew about me):

> il fuoco che non si smorza
> per me si chiamò: l'ignoranza.

> the fire that is not put out
> for me was called: ignorance.

From "Mediterraneo":

> Non sono
> che faville d'un tirso. Bene lo so: bruciare
> questo, non altro, è il mio significato.

> I am
> but sparks from a thyrsus. I know well: to burn,
> this, and nothing else, is my meaning.

From "Crisalide" (Chrysalis):

> Penso . . .
> al rogo
> morente che s'avviva
> d'un arido paletto, e ferve trepido.

> I think . . .
> of the dying fire
> which is revived
> by a dry small pole, and burns trembling.

These are all crucial moments for the poet's self-awareness: starting unwarily from the unkown notes of his flute in "Minstrels," he will arrive at the splendid results of "the burnt one" par excellence, "Arsenio." It should also be noted that the choice of "Minstrels," besides being determined (occasion-spur) by Debussy's piece performed at the 1917 concert, can and perhaps should be interpreted as a reflection or meditation by Montale on the role of the poet in today's society: if we listen to the Benjamin of the essay on Baudelaire, the climate has become increasingly inhospitable for modern poetry, because the lyric poet "has ceased to represent the poet *per se*. He no longer is a [bard] as Lamartine still was; he has become a representative of a [marginal and hardly tolerated] genre."[54]

But meanwhile Montale develops the motif of the heart, already metonymic of poetry being born, in another poem even more Debussyan than "Minstrels," that is, "Corno inglese," the only one retained from the "Accordi" suite from the very beginning, without hesitation or second thoughts. It is by far the major poetic achievement of the young Montale.

> Il vento che stasera suona attento
> —ricorda un forte scotere di lame—
> gli strumenti dei fitti alberi e spazza
> l'orizzonte di rame
> dove strisce di luce si protendono
> come aquiloni al cielo che rimbomba
> (Nuvole in viaggio, chiari
> reami di lassù! D'alti Eldoradi
> malchiuse porte!)
> e il mare che scaglia a scaglia,
> livido, muta colore,
> lancia a terra una tromba
> di schiume intorte;
> il vento che nasce e muore
> nell'ora che lenta s'annera
> suonasse te pure stasera
> scordato strumento,
> cuore.[55]

> The wind that tonight plays attentive
> —it reminds of a strong shaking of plates—
> the instruments of the thick trees and sweeps
> the copper horizon
> where strips of light stretch out
> like kites toward the sky that resounds
> (Traveling clouds, clear
> realms up above! Of high Eldorados
> unclosed doors!)
> and the sea which scale by scale,
> livid, changes color,
> thrusts to the shore a whirl
> of twisted foams;
> the wind that is born and dies
> in the hour that slowly darkens

> wish it played you too tonight,
> forgotten/untuned instrument,
> heart.

This brief composition contains many data of Montale's Debussyan experience, from the very title, an echo of the musician's predilection for the English horn,[56] to the precise thematic references to the two piano preludes "Le vent sur la plaine" and "Ce qu'a vu le vent de l'Ouest" and to the third part of the symphonic poem *La mer*, "Le dialogue du vent et de la mer." But these data are transcended and fused into a structure which is already, entirely and powerfully, Montalean—beginning with the metaphoric value of the title, wholly confirmed by a translation Montale made of Emily Dickinson's "The Storm" in 1945: "There came a wind like a bugle" is rendered in Italian as "Con un suono di corno / il vento arrivò."[57] The thematic importance of "Corno inglese" derives from the fact that the noun "wind" on which it is based is the very first of the entire oeuvre in verse, the beginning of "In limine" (On the threshold), the introductory poem of *Ossi*.[58]

> Godi se il vento ch'entra nel pomario
> vi rimena l'ondata della vita.

> Enjoy it, if the wind entering the apple-orchard
> brings back the wave of life.

This beginning emblematically defines not only the liminality of Montale's poetry,[59] but its double poetic space, the inner and the external, according to the by now classic schema by Juri Lotman, so important to understand the poetic text.[60]

Above all, this beginning presents the dynamic and creative function of the wind in Montale's poetry as absolutely primary. In this connection, one should read again the beautiful pages devoted by M. H. Abrams to "The Correspondent Breeze: A Romantic Metaphor,"[61] where the critic points out the frequency of words like "wind, breath,

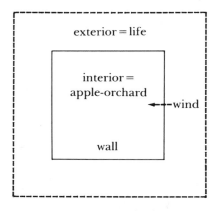

1. Space in "In limine."

blow" in the high romantic English poetry; he describes
their effect on the poet's "harp" or "Aeolian lyre" in that
they cause "a renewal of life and emotional vigor after ap-
athy and a deathlike torpor, and an outburst of creative
power following a period of imaginative sterility." Abrams
traces the origins and the history of this topos in both pa-
gan and Christian literature, of which romantic poetry is a
lay, secularized version—"yet the religious element re-
mains as at least a formal parallel, or a verbal or rhetorical
echo." Finally he vindicates the specificity of the romantic
wind in that Coleridge, Wordsworth, and Shelley make it
"peculiarly apt for the philosophical, political, and aes-
thetic preoccupations of the age," namely organicism, rev-
olution, and creativity.[62]

I have no doubt that Montale takes up or echoes the ro-
mantic topos of the inspiring wind, adapting it to his own
sensitivity and culture (the Debussyan filter is itself signifi-
cant).[63] It is the wind that in "In limine" makes possible "il
commuoversi dell'eterno grembo" (the moving of the eter-
nal womb), the transformation of the "pomario" (apple-or-
chard) into a "crogiuolo" (crucible); it is the wind that

causes a "rovello" (rage), as well as a desire to proceed and save others:

> Cerca una maglia rotta nella rete
> che ci stringe, tu balza fuori, fuggi!

> Look for a broken mesh in the net
> which grips us, jump out, flee!

One cannot sufficiently emphasize the salvific valence of Montale's poetry, his precise intentionality which structures so much of his poetic work toward that end.[64] I shall only quote a paradigmatic example from the later "Casa sul mare" (House by the sea), where the "passaggio" (passage) beyond the "varco" (opening) and the "via di fuga" (path to flight) singularly echo the exhortation of "In limine" (and the passage, the passing, is certainly the fundamental element of liminality, both poetic and anthropological):

> Penso che per i più non sia salvezza,
> ma taluno sovverta ogni disegno,
> passi il varco, qual volle si ritrovi.
> Vorrei prima di cedere segnarti
> codesta via di fuga
> labile come nei sommossi campi
> del mare spuma o ruga.
> Ti dono anche l'avara mia speranza.[65]

> I think that for most men there is no salvation,
> but someone may subvert every design,
> pass through the opening, find himself as he wanted.
> I'd like, before yielding, to point out for you
> this path of flight
> fleeting as in the stirred fields
> of the sea foam or furrow.
> I give you even my meager hope.

But in the meantime, keeping firmly in mind the valence and the intention made explicit by the wind, let us go back to "Corno inglese." It is a poetic construction containing a seascape, an affective experience, and a musical moment, all fused in an extraordinary unity. It is a small concentrate, a self-sufficient microcosm of Montale's themes, images, and techniques, in a circular structure which closes upon itself at the phonic, lexical, and syntactic levels.

At the phonic level, "Corno inglese" is entirely played on the contrast-complement (dissonance-harmony) between on the one hand the sibilant and fricative sounds (onomatopoetic or at least suggestive of the wind) of the consonant groups *s*, *st*, *str*, and *zz* (*st*a*s*era, *s*uona, *s*cotere, *str*umenti, *s*pazza, orizzonte, *s*uona*ss*e, *st*a*s*era, *s*cordato, and *str*umento), and on the other hand, the sounds of the nasal, labial, and dental groups e*nt* and o*mb*a (ve*nt*o, atte*nt*o, strume*nt*i, orizzo*nt*e, the variant prote*nd*ono at the beginning of the poem, ri*mb*o*mb*a and tro*mb*a in the middle, and then ve*nt*o, le*nt*a, and strume*nt*o at the end).

This dissonance-harmony is resolved in the liquid sound of the final "cuore"—and incidentally, there might be a Stravinskyan suggestion, too, in this contrastive-harmonic structure: to limit the influence of the new music to Debussy alone would wrong Montale.

The phonic texture of the poem, compact in its repetitions, is the musical basis for the lexical-semantic level, which is in turn itself oriented toward the specific area of musicality: "plays" and "wish it played," "instruments" on the second line and "instrument" on the penultimate seem to attract other signifiers, such as "resounds" and "whirl," which are obviously used for different signifieds ("tromba," in particular, means "trumpet" as well as "whirl"). In their turn, the sememes "the wind" (repeated twice, on the first and fourteenth lines), "the sea," and "the horizon" refer to a very simple spatial situation, which is defined temporally by "tonight" on the first and sixteenth lines, but is above all interiorized and related to the final and intensely affective vocative, "heart." At this level, the visual, pictorial power of Montale's poetry should also be emphasized, because it completes and intertwines with the evident musicality of segments like "a strong shaking of plates" or "the instruments of the thick trees": one thinks of the images "copper horizon / where strips of light stretch out / like kites," "traveling clouds," "the sea which scale by scale, / livid, changes color," and "a whirl of twisted foams."

The preciosity of certain lexical choices should then be noted: "scotere," "scaglia" (referred to the sea, as in "Meriggiare"),[66] "intorte"; certain plurals seem derived from Giacomo Leopardi and contribute to the poetic vagueness of the composition ("nuvole, reami, Eldoradi, porte"); and above all we should emphasize the ambiguity of "scordato," which, with its overlapping meanings of "discordant" or "untuned" and "forgotten" referred both to "strumento" and "cuore," overcomes the "crepuscolarismo" inherent in the final sememe. In fact, the sort of masked paronomasia resulting from the linking of *scordato* and *cuore*, both of which contain the sound of the title, *corno*, seems almost to suggest, without asserting it, that the poetic voice remains in the end dis*cor*dant.

The unity of the composition is further stressed by the numerous rhymes, internal rhymes and quasi-rhymes (or imperfect rhymes):

> vento attento strumenti protendono
> lame rame
> rimbomba tromba
> porte intorte
> colore muore cuore
> vento lenta strumento
> s'annera stasera.[67]

Above all, one should note the great effectiveness of the rhyme of "attento" (first line) and "strumento" (penultimate line): it is the most deliberate, the most intellectual of all, and is used to bring the beginning of the poem back to its conclusion, to make the wind and the heart, nature and the poetic voice resound again together, with an echo effect which attenuates the circular closure of the poem (one is reminded of Shelley's final invocation of the wind, in "Ode to the West Wind": "Make me thy lyre, even as the forest is").[68]

All the phenomena of the phonic and lexical levels examined so far can be grouped, as Morton Bloomfield does when he expands an insight by Roman Jakobson, in the category of linguistic repetition which has a high metonymic or contextual function, that is, it serves to call the reader's attention to poetic language as such (intransitivity).[69] At the syntactic level, for the first time in Montale's work, we see a poem construed on a single sentence, as will be the case with the later "L'anguilla" (The eel) in *La bufera*. This sentence is undoubtedly "a rhythmic, musical unit,"[70] and could be transcribed graphically in order to reveal its structure visually.

The principal sentence is the equivalent of the melodic line in a musical composition, and the secondary clauses are the harmonic materials; the relationship between the two syntactic elements is unbalanced, favoring the latter, whereby a new and different rhythm is created in the structure of the poem, a rhythm that can be clearly perceived even visually in the schema below (fig. 2). It is a single sentence whose syntax is rhetorically repetitive and suspended, carrying a great poetic effectiveness: the declarative clause "the wind thrusts to the shore a whirl of twisted foams" becomes an optative clause, "wish it played you too, heart."

Of course, it is also possible to interpret the syntax of the poem in the sense that it is "the sea" that "thrusts to the shore a whirl":[71] in this case there would be a principal sentence in the optative mood only, and with the subject repeated twice. The latter interpretation is tempting for its linearity, but seems less persuasive than the one I have highlighted, because it takes away dramatic force from the very wind which is the grammatical subject, the occasion of

Principal Sentence                    Secondary Clauses

The wind

that   plays the trees

—shaking of plates—

and sweeps   the horizon

where strips
stretch out
toward the sky

that resounds

(clouds,
Eldorados)

and the sea

that changes color

thrusts
a whirl;
the wind

that   is born

and dies in the hour

that darkens

wish it played

you too, heart.

2. Syntax of "Corno inglese."

the poem, the antagonist of the poet. Such an interpreta-
tion also does not account for the fact that, at the strictly
syntactical level, two verbs linked paratactically by a
comma (a comma, furthermore, which was added only in
the definitive edition: "the sea . . . changes color, thrusts
. . .") are certainly unusual in Montale; and finally, in the
description of another sea storm, the later one of "Ar-
senio," it is again the wind that predominates, grammati-
cally, over the sea: the "tromba di piombo, alta sui gorghi"
(laden whirl, high over the waves) is a "salso nembo vorti-
cante, soffiato dal ribelle elemento alle nubi" (salty, whirl-
ing spray, *blown* by the rebellious element toward the
clouds).

Yet, what actually matters is exactly the possibility of the
double interpretation, just as in the case of the "scordato
strumento" at the lexical-semantic level: it is a specific case
of that "syntactic ambiguity" which according to Bloom-
field is a poetic device capable of calling our attention to
the context, to make us "hesitate on it" and make us aware
of its "intransitivity," which forbids an early jump toward
the "referential meaning" of the single words taken indi-
vidually.[72]

In this context, which is made even more metonymically
poetic by the ambiguous syntax, all the numerous second-
ary and even incidental clauses are governed by the only
subject, "the wind," in a "Chinese box" structure culminat-
ing in the central parenthetic segment (in what might be
called a syntactic oxymoron). This segment between pa-
rentheses is a nominal sentence, without a verb, but clearly
related to the subject and the object of the principal clause:
the clouds are traveling, blown by the wind, as if, accord-
ing to the heart, they had their final destination in the high
Eldorados (which, incidentally, recall "le trombe d'oro
della solarità," the golden trumpets of solarity of "I li-
moni," also linked by "malchiuse porte" and "malchiuso
portone"). The nominal clause can be perceived as a true
musical phrase in the major (notice "clear, high, up above,"

and the two exclamation points) in dissonance or contrast
with the rest of the composition in the minor (with the con-
notations "copper, livid, twisted, darkens").

Therefore, the parenthetic sentence becomes the syntac-
tic, visual, musical, and affective focus of the whole poem:
it produces a fundamental dissonance, underlined and
contained by the parentheses which lengthen the already
wide distance between the subject and the object, between
nature and the poet. Another indication of this dissonance
can be found at the metrical level, in which the free use of
traditional verses ranges from the hendecasyllable to the
final senarius ("scordato strumento") and two-syllable line
("cuore"), both of which are rather unusual in the canon
of Italian lyric poetry.[73]

"Corno inglese" expresses for the first time, but in a less
dramatic tone, the same situation that will be developed
completely and emblematically in the later "Arsenio": in
the dialogue between immobility and movement, between
the poet and the world, the central parenthetic sentence
overcomes the potentially tragic connotations; it is an
opening on and of the imagination, hope, and *Sehnsucht* of
the poet who contemplates the storm, "the whirl of twisted
foams." The parentheses enclose (are) a "varco," the open-
ing Montale points out and wishes in "In limine,"[74] and the
one perhaps found by Esterina, the Debussyan "jeune fille
aux cheveux de lin," in "Falsetto": she is "come spiccata da
un vento" (as if blown by a wind), the poet is "della razza
di chi rimane a terra" (of the race of the ones who remain
ashore).

In "Corno inglese" we are dealing with an imaginary
opening, a conceptual and hypothetical one, which, how-
ever, is there, present and inviting, actualized by the invo-
cation at the center of the poem born from the Debussyan
and Ligurian music of the wind.[75] The wind which, at the
denotative-mimetic level, causes the stormy whirl, is also
the wind which, at the connotative-expressive level, ac-
cording to the wish of the poet should produce a music

capable of moving the untuned instrument of the heart. In any case, Montale does not describe a seascape and does not simply express a state of mind; he tries, through the poetic devices we have examined, to tear the appearances, to rip the veil, to reach (like Debussy, like Mallarmé) something essential. That his is an effort, and not an achievement, is inherent in the optative and parenthetic expression. "Corno inglese" is the moment of greatest fusion between poetry and music in Montale, the moment when the occasion-music is transformed, truly and definitely, into poetry.

# 2 | Ut Figura Poesis

Phrases came. Visions came. Beautiful pictures. Beautiful
phrases. But what she wished to get hold of was that very jar on
the nerves, the thing itself before it has been made anything.
VIRGINIA WOOLF, *To the Lighthouse*

## Poetry and Painting

The musicologist and art collector Luigi Magnani tells an
anecdote about a visit to his Roman house by Giorgio Mo-
randi:

> After having carefully looked at a small painting on
> the fireplace in the library, . . . he said, "This is per-
> haps the most beautiful painting you have here." This
> judgment could not sound very flattering to my ears,
> but it should have been so for the author of that paint-
> ing, which I handed to Morandi so that he could read
> in the back, under the dedication, the signature of Eu-
> genio Montale.

This anecdote is used by Magnani to emphasize the "al-
most exclusive predilection" Morandi had for "the kind of
painting in which he could recognize himself": "In fact
that painting, the work of a genial dilettante, showed an

intimate correspondence with Morandi's poetic vision, because of its essential structure and sober tones."[1]

Of course I do not wish to underestimate the documentary and interpretive importance, for the literary critic, of Montale's pictorial work. Suffice it to think that the poet himself, in "L'arte povera" (The poor art) from *Diario del '71*, evokes the prevailing colors of his paintings ("Vino e caffé, tracce di dentrificio," wine and coffee, smears of toothpaste) and the occasional materials on which they were painted (such as "carta blu da zucchero o cannelé da imballo," blue paper once used to wrap sugar, or paper for packaging); he has also drawn an interesting conclusion:

> E' la parte di me che riesce a sopravvivere
> del nulla ch'era in me, del tutto ch'eri
> tu, inconsapevole.[2]

> It is the part of me that succeeds in surviving
> out of the nothingness that was in me, of the whole
>   that was
> you, unaware.

A critic has justly noted that Montale's thematization of his own painting, his artistic activity that was "the least engaged, entirely marginal," and his transforming it into "a metaphor of his entire existence as man and artist, is characteristic of the 'soft-voiced' Montale at his best. The path of negation leads to the discovery of differential values."[3] Nevertheless, once we have recognized the existential and artistic importance of the paintings by the genial dilettante Eugenio Montale, it is time to devote some attention to the subject of the present research. This subject is not the correspondence of Montale's pictorial works with his poetry on the one hand, and with Morandi's paintings on the other; it is the homology between poetry and the visual arts, and particularly between the early poems of *Ossi di seppia* and Morandi's etchings.

To deal with this subject I go back first to the "imaginary

interview" from which we started, and which is the most explicit statement of the young poet's interest in modern painting. But my treatment will be different from that of Debussy's music: I wish to approach the question by starting not from a textual verification or a historiographic documentation, but from general considerations of a theoretical nature. First of all, there is a methodological hypothesis: it is possible to compare literature and the visual arts as texts, as modeling systems that are autonomous in themselves but also parts—and homologous parts—of that other modeling system we call culture.[4] On the one hand, such a hypothesis implies the obvious acknowledgment of the great interest painting has always provoked among writers;[5] on the other, with its emphasis on methodology, it tries (at least partially) to obviate whatever too subjective or unsystematic has been presented so far on the subject.[6] But the possibility of such a comparison should not be taken lightly, because the literary and the visual texts are normally "read" in different ways (the former in a syntagmatic progression, the latter by scanning, with pauses and accentuations in the eye's trajectory);[7] and because the metalanguages of art criticism and literary criticism differ as well (the former is ostensive and oblique, unlike the latter).[8]

Before I state my position, I wish briefly to discuss some major contemporary contributions toward a development of the comparison between literature and the visual arts. I shall begin with two books, *Études sémiologiques* by Louis Marin and *Discourse, figure* by Jean-François Lyotard.[9] Marin is perhaps more indirect than Lyotard in his approach, which is aimed primarily at a transcoding of the pictorial text into the metalanguage of criticism, but because of the linguistic basis of this metalanguage, the possibility for the comparison between painting and literature is strongly affirmed. Furthermore, he is interested in the ideological and narrative qualities of painting (as demonstrated by his analyses of Philippe de Champagne and

Poussin).[10] Marin uses a decidedly linguistic-semiotic approach: he speaks of pictorial syntagmatics, figures which are also units of meaning; of paradigmatics, stylistics and thematics of a painting; of pictorial codes (for example, in the analogic code of iconic painting the distinction between meaning and reference is masked [p. 29]); and of elementary structures of pictorial meaning, based upon the relationships among differential elements, for example, the polarized semantic axes (p. 39). Whether we speak of "symbolic" or "referential" works of art, we have to insist on the fact that "every pictorial object is truly such only when that opposition is superseded in the total unity of the work" (p. 42); therefore we can speak of the work as a "hypersign" (although Marin does not use such a term), which has to be considered in its "absolute autonomy" and as "designating only itself" (p. 34). Clearly, Marin performs a reading and an interpretation of pictorial texts.

By contrast, Lyotard is more radical than Marin: he plunges directly into the comparison between visual arts and literature, and privileges poetry rather than fiction. Above all he uses a deconstructive approach which reverses traditional notions.[11] Pursuing a well-known Derridean polemic, Lyotard says that we have difficulty in seeing the figural because we are accustomed to reading the discursive (p. 218). We have to recognize that painting is *not* like language; on the contrary it is language "inhabited by figures" (pp. 250-83). "Poetic language obeys not a generative grammar" of the kind we have seen in musical language according to Bernstein's interpretation, but "another order of production of meaning" (p. 310), the same order, precisely, that governs figural space. It is the order of the unconscious, of a phantasmatic matrix which is invisible but produces figure-forms and figure-images exactly like *poetical figures* in which the fundamental laws of language are rejected (see pp. 311-12 for a "reasonable table of poetic follies," compiled after the British linguist H. G. Widdowson). In every work of art, then, there is an oscillation, a tension between discourse and figure, between the realistic and the imaginary: its dimension as play depends precisely on the insertion of what is serious, linguistic, tied, within the element of difference, of free mobility (p. 382).

It is interesting to note that Wolfgang Iser, starting from completely different assumptions from Lyotard's, arrives at exactly the same conclusion concerning literary texts, when he says that "as the gestalt of the imaginary, fiction cannot be defined as counter-factual to existing realities. Fiction reveals itself as a product of the imaginary insofar as it lays bare its fictionality, and yet it appears to be a halfway house between the imaginary and the real."[12] But even more interesting—indeed, striking—is that Gilbert Durand preceded Lyotard by a decade in advocating a revaluation of the imaginary, not within a deconstructive strategy of re-inscription but by pursuing an anthropological inquiry.[13] Durand asserts that figural meaning always comes before conceptual meaning: space is the a priori form of the imaginary, and its qualities of ocularity, depth, and ubiquity concur in enhancing its "euphemistic function" against the putrefaction of death, because they cause ambivalence (p. 411). However, even if this space of the imaginary is primary for Durand, it is nonetheless necessary to retrace the trajectory between the semasiologic level of symbols and the semiotic level of discourse (the formalism of logic). This trajectory, this passage, is made possible by rhetoric, "intermediary between the imaginary and reason," which "supersedes the restrictions of logic through a series of the imaginary's bastard proceedings" (p. 421):

> The elementary translation of every rhetoric is nothing but the Euclidian property of translation, because rhetoric, like logic, expresses and thinks itself in terms of space. Just as space is the form of the imaginary in its struggle against destiny, so metaphor is its process

of expression, the power of the spirit, whenever it
thinks, to renew its terminology, to snatch it from its
etymological destiny. (p. 422)

Durand's statement that space is the a priori form of the
imaginary should be usefully integrated with E. H. Gom-
brich's research on visual arts: this research is supported
by Karl Popper's scientific, dynamic concepts and leads to
a consideration of perception as an active process, of the
type we have seen at work in the first chapter, in connec-
tion with the impressionists' technique; this process implies
memory and anticipation as well, and unfolds entirely be-
tween the opposite poles of redundancy and constraint—
the elements of the artistic message studied especially in
semiotics (the former) and in aesthetics (the latter).[14]

In any case, Durand's conclusions could appropriately
be related to a recent "plea for visual thinking" made by
Rudolf Arnheim, as well as to Pierre Francastel's "figura-
tive thought": they are all based on the preeminence of the
spatial and its interaction with expression (or logic, dis-
course, or language).[15] This preeminence is also vigorously
asserted by W.J.T. Mitchell, who expands Joseph Frank's
notion of "spatial form" in modernist literature and makes
of it "a crucial aspect of the experience and interpretation
of literature in all ages and all cultures" (he even suggests
the use of the adjective "tectonic" instead of "spatial" in
order to stress the visual and structural approach of his
proposal).[16] Finally, I should mention a contribution by
Marc-Eli Blanchard, who reaffirms the priority of descrip-
tion over narrativity, because description is the area where
the dialectics between language and desire is most remark-
able.[17]

It seems clear that a great effort in contemporary
thought is devoted to reassess, to clarify, and to unify the
basic modes of expressing, understanding, and communi-
cating man's experience. In such a cognitive process, the
inquiry into "the language of images" in general and more

particularly into the homology of literature and painting is central, and is causing a thorough questioning of such notions as the imaginary and the discursive, or the intuitive and the intellectual, or the figural and the logical, as well as of the ontological foundations on which these notions are based and their operational functions.

I think that the primacy of the imaginary has to be recognized and accepted, and we should also take into account its archetypal qualities (here Durand's Jungianism appears more promising than Lyotard's Freudianism). Such a recognition should help to correlate poetry and painting (or any other forms of art) as expressions of culture. For this attempt semiotics seems to be an indispensable, but not exclusive, tool. In fact, semiotics recognizes that, in Lotman's words, "The special character of visual perception inherent to man is such that visible spatial objects serve as the denotata of verbal signs; as a result verbal models are perceived in a particular way. The iconic principle and a graphic quality are wholly peculiar to verbal models as well."[18] The iconic principle and a graphic quality are visual, spatial characteristics which are primary (Durand would say that they are *the* imaginary) and which as such "inhabit" verbal models, including rhetoric. Once and because such primacy is recognized, then the language of the figural can be explored in its component parts, laws, and governing mechanisms, and finally transcoded into the metalanguage of a criticism that brackets metaphysics and considers itself as an operational, cognitive moment in the search for a description and definition of culture.

The preceding considerations should clear the way for my second presupposition, which actually is a historical concern: although I am not particularly keen on periodization, I do recognize the importance of certain broadly defined cultural periods.[19] Eugenio Montale was born in 1896 and died in 1981; Giorgio Morandi was born in 1890 and died in 1964; they belong to the same generation and share the same European culture of the beginning of this century and the same Italian tradition culminating (for instance and in particular) in the reviews *La Voce*, a vital presence until 1916, *La Ronda* (1919-22), and *Valori plastici* (1918-22).[20] We are clearly dealing with the crucial years for the formation and the beginnings of the two artists.

My third presupposition is a value judgment: I consider Montale as a great twentieth–century poet and Morandi as an equally great contemporary painter and engraver; few literary critics and, I believe, few art critics would dispute such a judgment.[21] However, the implication is that I privilege the relationship between Montale and Morandi above others that are equally possible but perhaps less significant. An example might be the following, suggested by Montale himself: Dino Campana's orphic poetry

> coincides with the beginnings in Italy of a metaphysical painting (Carrà, De Chirico), whose presence and intentions could not be ignored by Campana. Like the early De Chirico, Campana, too, is a suggestive evocator of Italian cities: Bologna, Faenza, Florence, Genoa flash in his poems and inspire some of his highest moments. Perhaps his "barbaric" or if you prefer ancient aspect is an indication of Campana's latent hearkening back to [the *fin de siècle* neo-classical poet] Giosuè Carducci?[22]

An indirect reply to Montale's question is given by the art critic Maurizio Calvesi, who, in documenting De Chirico's cultural formation in a Florence dominated by Giovanni Papini, establishes a precise relationship D'Annunzio-Campana-De Chirico, thus retrieving D'Annunzio's *Le città del silenzio* (The cities of silence), forgotten—deliberately?—by Montale.[23] Aside from Montale's anti-Dannunzian coherence (the reasons for his Debussyan choice should be recalled in this context), the relationship between the "imagific" poet, the "orphic" poet, and the "metaphysical" painter is certainly significant for an entire area of Italian (European) culture. But this area is antithetical to both Montale's and Morandi's. Hence we should mention at least some other, more congenial, possible relationships, before proceeding: for instance, Montale-De Pisis (which would be authorized also by a poem in *Le occasioni*), or Montale-Carrà (because of their Tyrrenian and possibly "metaphysical" themes),[24] or, on the other hand, Morandi-Cardarelli (in 1929 Morandi illustrated with twenty-two drawings a collection of Cardarelli's poems and prose pieces, *Il sole a picco*, but their "classicism," rooted in *La Ronda*, could be too easily misunderstood or overemphasized).[25]

The fourth presupposition is a thematic, formal, and epistemological choice: among the many possible aspects of the Montalean and Morandian works, I have emphasized their insistence on objects (cuttlefish bones, bottles) and landscapes (Ligurian sea coast, Apennines slopes and houses). They play a very precise role in their respective artists' organization of their art and view of man and the world.

Of course I am not the first (and perhaps shall not be the last) to make the connection between Montale and Morandi. For instance, during his visit to some American universities in 1959 Italo Calvino stated, in a clearly discursive manner:

> The rigor of Montale's poetry, the rigor of Giorgio Morandi's paintings, those still lifes of bottles in which the cold exactness of light envelops the humble reality of things, the rigor of Romano Bilenchi's fiction, the absolute dryness of his meager provincial stories; this was our inheritance from their "hermeticism." It is not a meager inheritance: Montale, Morandi, and Bilenchi taught us to hold to the essential in everything; they taught us that what we can be sure of is very little and must be endured to the very end. It was a lesson in stoicism.[26]

Calvino's statement is certainly peremptory, from a personal, a conceptual, and a historical viewpoint. I shall return to it later on, but for the moment let me quote a parallel assertion from an art critic, the late Francesco Arcangeli, perhaps the best interpreter of the Bolognese painter:

> Morandi, the latest chronologically in the great generation of Picasso, Braque, Carrà, and De Chirico, is the first, or among the first ones, in a generation of solitary explorers of the unknown: he belongs with Soutine, with Tobey, with Fautrier, with Eliot, with Montale. . . . Their poetics, whether figurative or nonfigurative, may be different from one another; but the sense of life in these men is analogous, as is their humble, but universally valid, inquiry into the ineliminable corners of existence, into the *hic et nunc*, a fistful of soil or a discarded cup, a meager nude or a cuttlefish bone, a galaxy or a distant city or a "waste land."[27]

More specifically, Arcangeli notes that in the twenties and early thirties "in Italy only Montale is closely akin to a Morandi he does not even know," and quotes such "programmatic lines from *Ossi di seppia* as "Non chiederci la parola che squadri da ogni lato / l'animo nostro informe" (Don't ask us for the word that squares / our formless soul from every side), "É ora di guardare le forme della vita che si sgretola" (It's time to look at the forms of a life that is crumbling), and "Codesto solo oggi possiamo dirti, / ciò che *non* siamo, ciò che *non* vogliamo" (All we can say today is / what we are *not*, what we do *not* want).

It seems clear from the preceding remarks that Calvino and Arcangeli link Montale and Morandi at a conceptual level and interpret their art as the carrier of a moral and epistemological "lesson"—that is, of a message conveyed through distinct but converging cultural codes, according to the dialogic principle by Bakhtin to which any conception of culture should always refer.[28] This principle has remarkable resemblances, or even a necessary integration, with the aesthetics of reception by Hans Robert Jauss and the Constance school,[29] not to mention Gombrich's theory of perception again. In fact, the parallel quotations from Calvino and Arcangeli clearly show that what happens in the addressee-reader of literary and figurative texts is projected also onto the forms of the perceived, artistic object: the correlation of a cultural system, which is at the same time a process of aesthetic sensitivity and of historical consciousness, establishes itself precisely in the active memory of the sympathetic addressee, even beyond the intentions of the artist-sender.

For my part, I accept such a correlation between Montale and Morandi as a preliminary point of departure, and shall proceed in my analysis by limiting the comparison to some etchings and some of the poems of *Ossi di seppia* only.[30] By delimiting the field of inquiry, I hope to have the advantage of specificity and to be able to explore the thematic and the formal levels of the cultural datum posited as a starting point.

## 2. Giorgio Morandi

Among contemporary Italian painters, Morandi is rightly famous for his still lifes and for being an engraver as well as a painter. Both characteristics are important. Marin says that a still life (a "nature morte") is a silent life which, however, speaks, and in examining the example of Chardin, one of Morandi's predecessors, he explains, "The revolutionary greatness of Chardin is that (by applying the canons of grand manner classical painting to still life) he has shown *pictorially* that beneath the socialized institution of codes of understanding and of valorization there lay a profound unity and autonomy of the pictorial order."[31] Marin also remarks that for Chardin objects are the "occasional pre-text" for the study of light and matter (p. 93). It is a very revealing coincidence that some of these words had already been used by Ardengo Soffici in a 1912 article in *La Voce* on painting in general (with the fundamental variation "*necessary* pretexts"), and that they return again in

Roberto Longhi and in Arcangeli (p. 27) to describe Morandi. In Longhi's words, "useless objects, unpleasant landscapes, seasonal flowers are the more than sufficient pretexts to express oneself 'through form'; and it is well known that one expresses only sentiments"; unlike the impressionists, Morandi uses these objects as "necessary symbols, terms ["vocaboli"] sufficient to avoid the shoals of absolute abstractness. This is so true that, from the same material pretext, he was able to render different sentimental timbres and to bend his grave, luminous elegy into ever-changing patterns."[32] The necessity of these pretexts (pre-texts) is fundamental for my analysis as well, because it dispels from the start any possible doubt about a purely formalistic conception of art, and of Morandi's art in particular.[33]

Morandi's art concentrates on objects and therefore it "discards the human figure," but such a "silence" is perhaps "the supreme homage of a by now desperate humanist to an image of man which is unrepeatable for the time being." In fact, modern art has been "unable to give anything but rhetorical, false, and hence short-lived images of man-the-hero, or at least of a man who is the master of himself and his destiny: here is a reason for Morandi's own destiny as a painter of landscapes and still lifes," says Arcangeli.[34] And another art critic, Lamberto Vitali, echoes, "If man is seemingly absent from [Morandi's] representations, they live, however, as functions of the human."[35] It should also be noted that still lifes constitute "a humble genre in comparison with sacred or historical subject painting."[36] Both epistemologically and formally, Morandi holds a very precise position, which is reinforced by his choice to work as an engraver (specifically, an engraver of etchings on copper or zinc plates).[37] In fact, the significance of his choice of the humble still life is heightened by his interest in etching, where color is discarded, and the inquiry into the nature of life and its forms is left entirely to black and white, to lines and surfaces. Besides, etching is also significant on another account: it is, as Benjamin has it, a typical "work of art in the age of mechanical reproduction," it is an art form par excellence in the modern world—and Morandi knew it.

The corpus of Morandi's etchings, collated and ordered by Vitali,[38] is impressive indeed: it is made up of 132 pieces, spanning from 1912 to 1956; of these, only five are portraits, only five deal with the human figure; all the others are still lifes and landscapes, and can be read as a macrotext, a long fidelity to a few fundamental themes subjected to an inexhaustible exploration through variation, one of the "mystical structures of the imaginary" according to Durand.[39] Furthermore, Amy Namowitz Worthen has correctly remarked that three-fourths of Morandi's etched works belong to the period 1927-1933: "In those years Morandi was forging his mature style and outlook. One is tempted to conclude that Morandi's uniquely personal vision was being formed and worked out primarily in the etchings. The rate of production in those years cannot simply be explained by his technical attraction to the medium, but rather by the excitement of the pursuit and creation of that vision of the *essence* of *forms*."[40] I believe that this explanation, which goes well beyond the years and the technical means in question, can also be used satisfactorily to justify my own choice of dealing with Morandi as an etcher: a synecdochic choice, in which truly the part stands for the whole.

Let us then look at, that is, read and interpret, some of these etchings.

First, a series of objects. Here is a *Still Life with Sugar Bowl, a Lemon, and Bread* (1921 or 1922, fig. 3): the temptation to quote Montale's "I limoni" is almost irresistible, but what really matters is Morandi's own *diminutio antiaulica* in his choice of these domestic objects and in his rendering of them through his "reticolo," a mesh or network of thin lines closely interwoven both in the foreground and in the background, leaving an area of white surfaces in the middle, clearly marked by the contours, but also softly

3. Giorgio Morandi, *Still Life with Sugar Bowl, a Lemon and Bread*, 1921 or 1922.

blended together by zones of *chiaroscuro* along the margins; the volumes stand out, the objects are there to be seen in front of us. This etching can be considered as one of the first and simplest examples of the many compositions on the same subject done by Morandi.

Here is a *Still Life with Bread Basket* (1921, fig. 4), in which *chiaroscuro* and perspective define the volumes, the tonality of light is subdued, the grouping of the objects on the table is seemingly random but actually carefully controlled, and the network of crisscrossing and parallel lines thickens and lightens. The interplay between white surfaces and dark ones, between *chiaroscuro* and perspective, between the grammar of the mesh and the syntax of the composition is also exemplified by the *Still Life with Drapery on the Left* (1927, fig. 5), in which it should be noted that

4. Giorgio Morandi, *Still Life with Bread Basket*, 1921.

5. Giorgio Morandi, *Still Life with Drapery on the Left*, 1927.

the "drapery on the left" is not a sumptuous drapery of the type we associate with a gothic or a baroque Madonna (on a paradigmatic axis), but is a small piece of cloth, perhaps a kitchen towel, hanging down the edge of the cabinet on which the bottles and the basket are placed, thereby contributing to the domestic scene and to its balance (on the syntagmatic axis). In short, this drapery is a good example of how a pictorial unit of meaning draws our attention to the autonomy of the pictorial order and its codes, of how we can read a pictorial text and interpret it in cultural terms.

Another stupendous variation is the *Large, Dark Still Life* (1934, fig. 6), which displays a tremendously minute network and is indeed "close and compact like a wall, on which a distant light barely filters through,"[41] and in which "the darkness has the function of excluding the viewer."[42]

6. Giorgio Morandi, *Large, Dark Still Life*, 1934.

By contrast, just as an example of objects as "necessary pretexts," here is the incredible luminosity of a late composition, *Still Life with Five Objects* (1956, fig. 7): they are *there*, immovable, silent, perfect in their materiality made of volume and light, yet mysterious, at the same revealing and concealing their essence. Perhaps a phenomenological analysis à la Merleau-Ponty could come close to Morandi's vision; or, better still, we could apply to the Bolognese painter Lyotard's words about Klee: "What Cézanne taught him is not a writing by geometric volumes, but the deconstruction of representation and the invention of a space of the invisible, the possible": these "objects" (figures-images) "attest that creation exceeds created nature" (p. 237); or again (and the multiplication of possibilities, of quotations, attests by itself to the inadequacy of the written word to render the visual image), one remembers Wallace Stevens's considerations:

7. Giorgio Morandi, *Still Life with Five Objects*, 1956.

The point is that the poet does his job by virtue of an effort of the mind. In doing so, he is in rapport with the painter, who does his job, with respect to the problems of form and color, which confront him incessantly, not by inspiration, but by imagination and by a miraculous kind of reason that the imagination sometimes promotes. . . . These works were *deliciae* of the spirit as distinguished from *delectationes* of the senses and this was so because one found in them the labor of calculation, the appetite for perfection.[43]

Finally, we should consider another type of variation, through which Morandi explores the nature of things: it is the different distances at which the viewer's eye is placed.

8. Giorgio Morandi, *Various Objects on a Table,* 1931.

For instance, the *Various Objects on a Table* (1931, fig. 8) are seen from afar, and they "could be distant hillside towns seen from a plain," while in the round and oval etchings of the forties "Morandi forces us to see the objects incompletely, by stealth, as though we peer through a keyhole unto a private world" (see for instance *Still Life in an Oval,* circa 1942, fig. 9).[44]

Let us turn now to a series of landscapes, beginning with the first of Morandi's graphic oeuvre, *The Bridge on the Savena River at Bologna* (1912, fig. 10). It may be less perfect than the other etchings we have seen so far, yet it already shows the search for the essential; it is a landscape without human figures, enclosed within the hard margins of the composition (the house on the left, the tree on the right, a strong diagonal emphasis). Deep and long straight lines (which are a prelude to the later network) effectively contrast the white surface of the road, the parapet, and the house walls. After indicating Vitale da Bologna and Cézanne among the "origins" of the early Morandi, Arcangeli comments that Morandi already "sees his own strong soli-

9. Giorgio Morandi, *Still Life in an Oval,* circa 1942.

10. Giorgio Morandi, *The Bridge on the Savena River at Bologna,* 1912.

tude even in this prosperous countryside near Bologna" (p. 25).

The continuity of Morandi's project and his ceaseless exploration are shown by a later landscape, *The White Road* (1933, fig. 11). The composition is very similar to that of the early *Bridge*, because of the long, diagonal, white space of the road, yet the innovations are equally memorable: the white spaces, of both the road and the sky, predominate here and actually govern the light grey masses of the houses, trees, bushes, and rocks, and dictate the fine mesh of the network of lines. Everything conjures up "the blinding light of that countryside, which seems to send back the echo of restless cicadas."[45] Throughout the numerous landscapes by Morandi we can trace the same syntagmatic choice of subject (Bologna and Grizzana, his "Mont Sainte-Victoire"[46]), and, on the paradigmatic axis, the same basic

11. Giorgio Morandi, *The White Road,* 1933.

execution through variation: tonalities of light achieved through the interplay of absolutely white surfaces and darker ones of a thick or loose mesh (or of markedly or softly etched lines), and always a tremendous mastery of the compositional elements: angle, spatial groupings, perspective, balance. Four examples will suffice here: *Landscape (House at Grizzana)* and *Landscape of Il Poggio* (both 1927), *Il Poggio in the evening* (1927, fig. 12), and *Il Poggio in the morning* (1928, fig. 13).

Based on the necessary pre-texts of his domestic objects and of familiar landscapes, the graphic language of Giorgio Morandi seems indeed to achieve a miraculous oscillation between the imaginary (perfection) and the real (representation). In its pictorial autonomy, this language conveys a cultural meaning, which Calvino called "stoic" and which we could also term antiromantic and antiheroic. This message is perhaps even more radical, in its subdued appearances, than that conveyed by the figurative and poetic topos of the minstrel or mountebank.

12. Giorgio Morandi, *Il Poggio in the Evening*, 1927.

Although he was tempted by the proposals of futurism, cubism, and the metaphysical painting of Carrà and De Chirico, quietly and stubbornly Morandi found his own way and established his own figurative code, which was unmistakable.[47] He drew on the accepted tradition (from Piero della Francesca to Vermeer, from Rembrandt to Cézanne) and posited his own "pure painting" which can be linked with, but must be distinguished from, the "abstract painting" of Mondrian.[48]

From the beginning, Morandi was the best representative of that "minority culture" or "minority civilization" indicated repeatedly by Arcangeli (also in connection with *La Voce*), which coincides with a particular stratum of Italian and European society, the *petite bourgeoisie*, the repository of values antithetical to fascism. In this context, we could even connect Morandi's belonging to the *petite bourgeoisie*, intended as a spiritual attitude, to Albert Camus's *L'homme revolté*, perhaps filtered through Giuseppe Raimondi, the Bolognese writer. But in the meantime it is important to emphasize, with Arcangeli, that Morandi, like Montale,

13. Giorgio Morandi, *Il Poggio in the Morning*, 1928.

could never have been a fascist, because there was in
him another unshakable truth: that of a modest, an-
cient, civilized Italy, still capable sometimes of pro-
found and serious things. He has not only sung "what
we are *not*, what we do *not* want," he has not only
avoided the human figure; but he has slowly come to
affirm an ascertained, a human possession of the
world and things. It is not much, but in it there is im-
plicit the whole. That is why Morandi is a teacher of
inner freedom as well as of civic behavior. (pp. 162-63)

In this extremely persuasive interpretation by Arcangeli, then, Morandi, as a contemplative *petit bourgeois*, became the masterly painter and engraver of still lifes and land-scapes; in so doing he made the radius of vision and that of conscience coincide, and achieved a difficult equilibrium between "the autonomy of art and the humanness of art" (pp. 288 and 305), or, again, between the imaginary and the real.

One last image from his etchings seems appropriate to link him with Montale: *The Garden at Fondazza Street* (1924, fig. 14). The garden, the orchard is the thematic image that recurs hauntingly throughout *Ossi*.

## 3. "Meriggiare pallido e assorto"

Let us turn, then, to Montale's poetry. My purpose is to emphasize the homologies to be found between certain po-

14. Giorgio Morandi, *The Garden at Fondazza Street*, 1924.

ems of *Ossi di seppia* and Morandi's etchings. Differences
exist, of course: for instance, in the critical terminology
used to describe visual arts there is no term yet comparable
to poetic "voice";[49] the *time* of Montale's poetry is indeed
unique and "unforgettable";[50] and more particularly, the
development of Montale from the stoicism of *Ossi* to the
skepticism of *Quaderno di quattro anni* or *Altri versi* does not
parallel a similar development in Morandi. But homolo-
gies do seem to be more interesting and important than
differences.

We might begin by stating that Montale's thematic and
semantic *diminutio antiaulica* is the poetic homologue of
Morandi's "humble genre" of etching still lifes and land-
scapes. The first stanza of "I limoni" is quite an appropri-
ate case in point:

> Ascoltami, i poeti laureati
> si muovono soltanto fra le piante
> dai nomi poco usati: bossi ligustri o acanti.
> Io, per me, amo le strade che riescono agli erbosi
> fossi dove in pozzanghere
> mezzo seccate agguantano i ragazzi
> qualche sparuta anguilla:
> le viuzze che seguono i ciglioni,
> discendono tra i ciuffi delle canne
> e mettono negli orti, tra gli alberi dei limoni.[51]

> Listen to me, the poets laureate
> move only among plants
> with little–used names: boxwood, cyprus, or acanthus.
> As for me, I love the roads that end up in grassy
> ditches where in half-dried
> puddles boys grab
> some meager eel:
> the little lanes which follow the ridges,
> slope down among the tufts of cannas
> and lead into orchards, amidst the lemon trees.

Not only are the lemon trees juxtaposed with acanthus
and other gloriously poetic vegetation, but all the images

of the stanza indicate the anti-Petrarchan and anti-Dannunzian stance of Montale, from the grassy ditches to the little lanes, from the half-dried puddles to the meager eel, from the tufts of cannas to the orchards. We should not take Montale's statement blindly: his poetry is *also* aulic, it does acknowledge and incorporate tradition into his own original voice (see "Io, per me," at the center of the stanza).[52] But the statement is important, nonetheless. As a matter of practical poetics, already it indicates the thematic choice and the lexical recurrence in *Ossi* of humble objects. Moreover, the sememes denoting objects are tied together in the texture of the poem by typically Montalean procedures, such as internal rhyme (bossi-fossi) and assonance (pozzanghere-mezzo-ragazzi-viuzze-ciuffi), alongside the canonical rhyme (ciglioni-limoni).

The very title of the poetic collection, *Ossi di seppia*, cuttlefish bones, refers to an inconspicuous object, but "this God-forsaken thing," as Cambon puts it, "loses its insignificance to become (as does the pebble) a symbol of essentialness."[53] Especially relevant in this connection are the images that appear in two comparisons—and it should be remembered that comparisons or similes are the simplest form of metaphor, that is, the linguistic device that transposes the imaginary into the verbal, the figural into the discursive. The first image is in "Mediterraneo":

Avrei voluto sentirmi scabro ed essenziale
siccome i ciottoli che tu volvi,
mangiati dalla salsedine;

I would have wanted to feel rough and essential
like the pebbles you roll,
gnawed by brackishness;

The second is in "Riviere":

Oh allora sballottati
come l'osso di seppia dalle ondate
svanire a poco a poco.

> Oh then tossed
> like the cuttlefish bone by the waves
> to vanish little by little.

"Like the pebbles," "like the cuttlefish bone": these two similes, these two images can be taken as guiding points for the many objects with a similar function to be found throughout *Ossi di seppia*, true and actual still lifes in poetry:

> muro d'orto
> (orchard wall),

> fuscello teso dal muro
> (twig stretching from the wall),

> l'agave sullo scoglio
> (the agave on the rock),

> un croco
> perduto in mezzo a un polveroso prato
> (a crocus
> lost in the middle of a dusty meadow),

> pochi stocchi d'erbaspada
> (a few stalks of spiky grass),

> casa sul mare
> (house by the sea),

> le petraie d'un greto
> (the stones of a river bed),

> il girasole col suo volto giallino
> (the sunflower with its light-yellow face),

> una reliquia di vita
> (a relic of life),

> la foglia riarsa
> (the parched leaf),

> la statua nella sonnolenza / del meriggio
> (the statue in the drowsiness / of noonday),

> la carrucola del pozzo
> (the pulley of the well),

sugheri alghe asterie
(corks seaweeds starfish),

i ciuffi delle aride canne
(the tufts of arid cannas),

l'erba grigia / nelle corti scurite, tra le case
(the grey grass / in darkened courtyards, amid
houses),

una statua dell'Estate / fatta camusa da lapidazioni
(a statue of Summer / made snub by stonings),

strada portico / mura specchi
(street arcade / walls mirrors),

rami cedui
(coppiced branches),

reti stinte
(discolored nets)

One could continue, but the given examples should suffice. As a commentary to this brief and incomplete list, let me quote Contini's considerations on the "descriptive" and "assertive" phases of *Ossi di seppia*: " 'Love' for things . . . is substituted for by a harsh statement of possession, through the insistence on the *presence*, on the *essence* of objects. . . . Underlying the whole of Montale's poetry there is a dramatic struggle of the poet with objects, almost in order to find a justification for *seeing*."[54] We immediately notice the intimate consonance of these remarks by Contini with Arcangeli's statement, previously quoted, that Morandi "has slowly come to affirm an ascertained, a human possession of the world and things": indeed, like the painter, the poet needs to find "a justification for *seeing*." That is why the many objects present in *Ossi di seppia* are an essential part of Montale's poetic texture. They are the figural that bursts into the discourse, the "necessary pretexts" for his poetry.

These same objects surround, accompany, or simply constitute one of the three major themes of his early book, which the author himself described as "landscape, love,

and evasion."[55] Clearly, landscape in the present context is
not only a major theme, but also a formal aspect which re-
lates Montale to Morandi most significantly. In fact, both
objects and landscape, by their very presence in the poetic
text, constitute a redimensioning of the human figure: the
voice of the poet acquires its value only through his rela-
tionship with external reality, which can only be perceived
through its appearances, its manifestations. Contingency
invites inquiry into essence. In this sense objects and land-
scapes are much more than "objective correlatives" of the
poet's inner situation.

The preeminence of the Ligurian landscape, then, im-
plies a certain disappearance of the human figure, al-
though this landscape remains a function of the human (as
the other two themes of love and evasion clearly indicate),
exactly as is the case in Morandi's etchings of the Bo-
lognese countryside. Nowhere in *Ossi di seppia* is this land-
scape or still-life function more apparent than in "Merig-
giare pallido e assorto":

Meriggiare pallido e assorto
presso un rovente muro d'orto,
ascoltare tra i pruni e gli sterpi
schiocchi di merli, frusci di serpi.

Nelle crepe del suolo o su la veccia
spiar le file di rosse formiche
ch'ora si rompono ed ora s'intrecciano
a sommo di minuscole biche.

Osservare tra frondi il palpitare
lontano di scaglie di mare
mentre si levano tremuli scricchi
di cicale dai calvi picchi.

E andando nel sole che abbaglia
sentire con triste meraviglia
com'è tutta la vita e il suo travaglio
in questo seguitare una muraglia
che ha in cima cocci aguzzi di bottiglia.

To rest at noon pale and absorbed
near a scorching orchard wall,
to listen amid bush and brake to
cracks of blackbirds, rustle of snakes.

In the soil cracks or on the vetch
to watch the lines of red ants
now breaking and now intertwining
on top of tiny stacks.

To observe through foliage the distant
palpitating of sea scales
while there rise quivering creaks
of cicadas from barren peaks.

And walking in the dazzling sun
to feel with sad astonishment
how all of life and its travail
is in this following a wall
which has on top jagged shards of bottle.

The first remark to be made about this poem concerns the semantic and the syntactic levels of the very first word, "meriggiare," posited "in a precarious balance between the status of verb and noun, set in a sentence apparently lacking a grammatical subject."[56] In fact, "meriggiare" may mean "noontimeness" or "to rest at noon," and is therefore another perfect example of Bloomfield's syntactic ambiguity, already noted in "Corno inglese," while at yet another level it is a proof of what Debenedetti calls "the non-obligatoriness of signifieds" in "hermetic" poetry.[57] As a signifier, then, "meriggiare" in any case does exclude a grammatical subject and, if we take it as a verb, it is the first in a series of other infinitive tenses, plus a gerund (andando), all of which "refer to human activities from which Man himself has been banished. They impose the act of seeing without a see-er, the act of listening without a pair of ears, of spying without an inquisitive mind to do the spying":[58] meriggiare, ascoltar, spiar, osservare, sentire, seguitare. Four of these infinitives are linked together also by internal rhyme, and one (spiar) by quasi-rhyme; and they are reinforced by another verb-noun (palpitare), which is a human activity referred to sea scales, the object of human vision. Not only thematically, but formally as well, this poem successfully removes the human figure from the scene and achieves the closest possible homology between poetic "voice" and pictorial "viewpoint."

This homology is further emphasized by other formal qualities of the text: just as in Morandi the Apenninian slopes, roads, and houses are formalized into compositions with tonalities of light (*chiaroscuro*, mesh, white surfaces, lines), so the Ligurian sea and landscape is transformed by Montale into "a series of phonetic clashes dominated by the close interaction of plosive and guttural consonants":[59] *pr*uni, ste*rp*i, s*chi*occhi, se*rp*i, scri*cch*i, also connected with labials: "tremuli scricchi / di cicale dai calvi picchi." On the lexical-semantic level, these phonetic clashes should be considered within the closely knit system of rhyme and assonance patterns: sterpi-serpi, schiocchi-scricchi-picchi, or later on, even more impressively, the sequence abbaglia-meraviglia-travaglio-muraglia-bottiglia. Nicolas Perella notes that the "trigrammatic *gli*" appears "almost in a vertical column," the visual image of the wall—"mura*gli*a"—into which it is inserted.[60] These patterns have little to do with an actual representation of the landscape itself; they are part of its poetical transcoding, which is valuable as such because of its sonorous texture, its phonetic form.

It is interesting to note that in this poetic landscape there is a criss-crossing, almost a mesh, of geometric planes: the horizontal (lines of ants, distant sea scales, walking, following a wall) and the vertical (stacks, peaks, dazzling sun, top of the wall) clearly constitute vectors which guide the reader's perception. But if such a geometry implies a geometer, it is not exactly a pictorial geometry, because it is governed by a peculiar perspective which allows the conjunction of the minutest detail (the red ants) with the vast horizon (the distant palpitating of sea scales) within the same composition—while for a painter (for example, Morandi) the distance of the object to be contemplated (to be "spied" on) may be now close, now far, but only in different compositions. Furthermore, in order to underline the specificity of poetry, we should think of the synesthetic copresence of sight and sound.

A possible key to an understanding of such a peculiar perspective is the syntax of the poem, in which conjunctions abound: presso (near), tra (amid), nelle (in the), su (on), a sommo di (on top of), tra (through), mentre (while), dai (from), con (with), in cima (on top). Durand notes that in the "mystic structure of the imaginary" there is a type of expression that tends to privilege precisely such prepositions, which try to establish some (metonymic) link between logically disparate objects. This type of expression belongs to the same "nocturnal regimen of the imaginary" already pointed out with reference to Morandi's repetition and variation, and it reinforces the comparison between the poet and the painter at a very basic, anthropological level, which even precedes their homology at the level of culture.[61]

The last stanza of the poem articulates a rational discourse from the series of visual and auditive perceptions transcribed so far, yet it is very significant indeed that such a rational discourse is introduced by the verb "sentire" (to feel) and culminates in a metaphor (living a life as following a wall). This metaphor means first of all that in expressing and communicating his experience of the world Montale uses the Ligurian landscape as a necessary pretext for a poetic discourse which is halfway between the real and the imaginary, between and betwixt, "on the edge."[62] But we should recall Jakobson's assertion that in poetry "any metonymy is slightly metaphorical and any metaphor has a metonymical tint"; we should also remember Bloomfield's idea that "poetry is a kind of syntactization of referential words. They become more metonymic and less metaphorical," so that "poetry has a syntactic as well as a semantic density."[63] Now we can see that this last Montalean metaphor is no exception to the rules of the two linguists. Perhaps Montale (like Morandi) devises series of metonymies from which he hopes a metaphor might be precipitated: we could speak of a "diegetic metaphor" (as Genette does for Proust),[64] to convey the sense in which the Montalean metaphor derives from the spatio-temporal context of the poem. Metaphor seems to appear as a kind of virtual, perfect point at which Montale aims, but which he does not claim he quite reaches. "The absolute expression," he says later, in the "imaginary interview" discussed in the first chapter, "remained an unreachable limit."[65] In his etchings, Morandi, too, uses an essentially metonymic process, and he too does not claim he has reached a perfection he continues to seek through his constant repetition and variation.

In the end, it has been possible to trace a trajectory in both Montale and Morandi that defines their respective works of art in terms of the imaginary and the discursive, and the definition implies both origin in the anthropological imaginary and expression through cultural codes and meanings, which were in fact properly received by generations of Italians, as is shown by Calvino's and Arcangeli's statements quoted earlier in this chapter. In particular, the metaphor-metonymy in the last stanza of "Meriggiare pallido e assorto" seems the most adequate and revealing conclusion for my analysis; and I might add, with all due irony and self-irony, that there is perhaps a sort of poetic (or should I say pictorial?) justice in the final image of the poem, which unites Montale's "wall" with Morandi's "bottle," the two "real" objects that are in turn the metaphors-metonymies of the two artists' unending pursuit of perfection.

# 3 | Strategies of the Antihero

Dove avete lasciato il vecchio fuoco,
delizia d'altri bardi?
Tarde e fioche le corde, il vostro suono
è forzato, le note sono poche!
WILLIAM BLAKE, *Alle Muse*,
Italian translation by Eugenio Montale

## Poetry and Prose

Starting from an analysis of the element of sound in the
early poetry of Eugenio Montale (especially in "Corno in-
glese"), I have proceeded with an examination of its visual
aspect (particularly in "Meriggiare pallido e assorto"). To
be more exact, from a comparison between poetry's
phonic level and the dissonance of Debussy's "new music"
I have arrived at a homology between the figurative level
of Montale's poetic lexicon and Morandi's etching lan-
guage. Actually, such an analysis presupposes a copres-
ence of levels, whose vertical stratification (the audible and
the visual coexist both in "Corno inglese" and "Merig-
giare") is not limited to the elements studied so far. It in-
cludes a third one, equally fundamental, and in fact im-
possible to put aside even if it was somewhat sacrificed. I
am referring to the discursive (or ideologic) element. Mon-

69

tale himself, incidentally, used to say that "the compromise between sound and meaning does not allow for partial solutions favoring the one or the other element."[1]

This element includes all the references to dissonance as a disharmony between self and world, and to the insistence on poetic objects rather than on the human figure, references that have a very precise thematic, symbolic, and cultural meaning: antiheroism as a choice of life, as a vision of the world. This ideologic element, this discursive level should then be given a greater attention than that provided so far. We might start with some general considerations on literary phenomenology: the intertextual homology between lyric poetry and narrative prose seems to have been too often sacrificed to the exigencies of rational clarity and genre classification inherent in historicist discourse.

Not by chance Pier Vincenzo Mengaldo, while recalling the "two seemingly contrasting theses" by Bakhtin on the "plasticity" of the novel and by Juri Tynianov on the "fluidity" of lyric poetry, advocates a two-pronged critical research. On the one hand, he proposes an analysis of "the decay of traditional forms of verse narration, in which *Don Juan, Pan Tadeusz* and above all *Eugene Onegin* are indeed the exceptions confirming the rule" (and we might certainly add Attilio Bertolucci's work). On the other, he suggests an examination of the various ways in which lyric poetry "has absorbed narrative and more generally prosaic requirements and modalities, with the related crises and formal adjustments." For his part, Mengaldo emphasizes the "narrativity" of Montale's poetry and notices that particularly in *Le occasioni* there is an "even more refined narrative pagination of existential myths. Montale builds it by inserting into the strictures of his lyric form precisely the suggestions of the best contemporary novelists (Proust, Svevo, the British) beside those of his favorite verse narrators like Browning."[2]

Another critic, Romano Luperini, also underscores the "decidedly narrative rather than musical slant" of the

"Mediterraneo" suite in *Ossi di seppia*. This slant includes "links connecting the various movements," "an existential balance sheet which presupposes a development, a temporal arc," "a subject positing himself as character . . . (almost an *n*th portrait of the artist as a young man)," and a final "meaning as a conclusion of his search for truth, for a sense of his life." Therefore, for Luperini "Mediterraneo" is a "fundamental chapter" in that "true novel of identity which is *Ossi di seppia*."[3] I wish to broaden and deepen both Mengaldo's and Luperini's remarks, and I wish to do so both in the direction of the history of the novel and in that of lyric poetry, with special emphasis on Montale, of course.

At the outset it should be remembered that in Bakhtin's conception the novel is the hegemonic genre of modernity, the one which, by continuously questioning itself and by adhering to a changing reality, promotes the "novelization of literature"; in doing so it frees the other literary genres from their sclerotic conventions: "The novelization of other genres does not imply their subjection to an alien generic canon [since 'the novel, after all, has no canon of its own']; on the contrary, novelization implies their liberation from all that serves as a brake on their unique development, from all that would change them along with the novel into some sort of stylization of forms that have outlived themselves."[4]

Furthermore, there are three areas in which the novel is opposed to the epic and which appear to be extremely relevant for lyric poetry as well: its "multilinguistic awareness" (polyphony, dialogic imagination, heteroglossia); its temporal and cognitive organization, centered on its "direct contact" with today's "developing reality"; and especially its way of constructing characters:

> The destruction of epic distance and the transferral of the image of an individual from the distanced plane to the zone of contact with the inconclusive events of the

present (and consequently of the future) result in a radical re-structuring of the image of the individual in the novel—and consequently in all literature. Folklore and popular-comic sources for the novel played a huge role in this process. Its first and essential step was the comic familiarization of the image of man. Laughter destroyed epic distance; it began to investigate man freely and familiarly; to turn him inside out, expose the disparity between his surface and his center, between his potential and his reality. A dynamic authenticity was introduced into the image of man, dynamics of inconsistency and tension between various factors of this image; man ceased to coincide with himself, and consequently men ceased to be exhausted entirely by the plots that contain them.

Bakhtin's last point deserves further consideration, especially because he stresses the role of popular masks (such as Pulcinella or Harlequin) in the formation of the novel out of folklore, and the functions of the rogue, clown, and fool in the development of a genre in which, paradigmatically, the epic hero "turns into a jester." In fact, in literary history, at least as far as the West is concerned, the figure of the hero has undergone a steady decline. Instead of the classic hero of the Greeks it has been possible to speak of modern and contemporary heroes who are "mediocre" or "middling" (Lukàcs), "passive" (Garber), "unheroic" (Giraud), "intellectual" or "impossible" (Brombert), "artistic" (Blackmur), "vanishing" (O'Faolain);[5] or, again, the modern hero has been defined as "comic" (Torrance), "absurd" (Galloway), "limping" (Hays), and "a failure" (Schilling).[6] Even Montale noticed, following Mario Praz, that "the everyday hero, the bourgeois hero is born" in the nineteenth-century novel,[7] while Luigi Pirandello peremptorily remarks, in his fundamental essay on *L'umorismo* (Humor): "The humorist does not recognize heroes; or better, he lets others represent heroes; for his part, he knows what a legend is and how it is formed, what history is and how it is formed: they are all compositions, more or less ideal compositions, which he enjoys taking to pieces. And one cannot say it is a pleasant amusement." In fact Pirandello must underscore "those unbecoming, loose, whimsical elements, all those digressions that are noticeable in a humoristic work, in contrast with the orderly mechanism, the *composition* of the work of art in general." With a significant choice, he hearkens back to the authority of Lawrence Sterne and concludes:

> The ordinary artist pays attention only to the body; the humorist pays attention to the body and the shadow, and sometimes more to the shadow than to the body; he notes all of this shadow's tricks, how it becomes now elongated, now large, almost as if it made grimaces to the body, which in the meantime does not take them into consideration and does not care about them. In medieval representations of the devil we find a scholar who, in order to mock him, makes him catch his own shadow on the wall. He who represented this devil was certainly not a humorist. A humorist knows very well how much a shadow is worth: Chamisso's *Peter Schlemihl* is a perfect example.[8]

I believe it is unnecessary to emphasize how valuable the above remarks are for understanding the mechanisms and meanings of Pirandello's oeuvre, a true milestone in contemporary theatre and fiction. It seems more useful, instead, to follow the reference to *Peter Schlemihl* (which, incidentally, was known to Montale as well).[9] Its protagonist, who sells his shadow to the devil and then expiates his guilt throughout his life, is posited as a kind of anti-Faust and is perhaps the best known of a whole series of similar figures, which are a specifically Jewish contribution to Western art.

Lionel Trilling and Hannah Arendt have emphasized the role of the Jewish comic in Western culture and fiction, especially through insistence on the body and on bodily

functions, even "low" ones (and here it is necessary to re-
call the homologous categories of the "carnivalesque" and
the "lower bodily stratum" put forth by Bakhtin in his
studies of Rabelais and Dostoevsky), not to mention the an-
tiheroism of the rabbinic tradition.[10] Heine's and Chamis-
so's Schlemihl is a "pariah" in the social world but he is also
a "lord of dreams" (the poet protected by Apollo), and the
same phenomenon occurs, even in a more aggressive man-
ner, in Kafka and his doubles—from K. to Gregor Samsa,
from Joseph to the hunger artist, men of good will who
might be any one and each of us. But the climax of the
Jewish tradition, in this sense, according to Arendt, is
Charlie Chaplin, who, although not himself Jewish, suc-
ceeded in representing the typically Jewish figure of the
harassed suspect:

> To be sure, he too is a *schlemihl*, but not of the old vi-
> sionary type, not a secret fairy prince, a protégé of
> Phoebus Apollo. Chaplin's world is of the earth earthy,
> grotesquely caricatured if you will, but nevertheless
> hard and real. It is a world from which neither nature
> nor art can provide escape and against whose slings
> and arrows the only armor is one's own wits or the
> kindness and humanity of casual acquaintances.
> . . . Chaplin's own childhood had taught him two
> things. On the one hand, it had taught him the tradi-
> tional Jewish fear of the "cop"—that seeming incarna-
> tion of a hostile world; but on the other, it had taught
> him the time-honored Jewish truth that, other things
> being equal, the human ingenuity of a David can
> sometimes outmatch the animal strength of a Goliath.
> . . . Chaplin's suspect is linked to Heine's *schlemihl* by
> the common element of innocence . . . , an expression
> of the dangerous incompatibility of general laws with
> individual misdeeds. Although in itself tragic, this in-
> compatibility reveals its comic aspects in the case of the
> suspect, where it becomes patent. There is obviously

no connection at all between what Chaplin does or does not do and the punishment which overtakes him. Because he is suspect, he is called upon to bear the brunt of much that he has not done. Yet . . . he is able to get away with a great deal. Out of this ambivalent situation springs an attitude both of fear and of impudence, . . . the kind so familiar to generations of Jews, the effrontery of the poor "little Yid."

. . . It was in this "little Yid," poor in worldly goods but rich in human experience, that the little man of all peoples most clearly discerned his own image.[11]

Therefore it is not by chance that the greatest Italian writer of Jewish origin, before choosing his definitive pseudonym, played with assonances and meanings in order to pass from his family name, Schmitz, through Schlemihl, to Samigli, his first literary screen.[12] And it is certainly not by chance that "Schlemihlism" runs, in more or less allusive, masked, and indirect ways, throughout his entire oeuvre. Here I wish to present a minimal example of such Schlemihlism. It is an extremely pertinent piece, because it concerns precisely the chain fear-suspicion-innocence as it is experienced by Zeno Cosini, Italo Svevo's Schlemihl:

We had started without letters of introduction, and many of the strangers we found ourselves among seemed to me hostile. It was an absurd fear, but I could not get over it. I might have been attacked, insulted or, what was worse, maligned, and who would have defended me? This fear became a positive panic, though fortunately no one, not even Augusta, found out about it. I was in the habit of buying almost every paper that was offered me in the street. One day when I was standing in front of a newsvendor's bench, it occurred to me that he might easily take a dislike to me and have me arrested as a thief, because although I had only bought one paper from him I had a number

under my arm still unopened, which I had bought
from other newspaper boys. I hurried away, followed
by Augusta, to whom I gave no reason for my sudden
haste.[13]

A similar situation, involving fear-suspicion-innocence, is
portrayed by another great writer of Jewish origin, Saul
Bellow: when Professor Herzog, the protagonist of the
eponymous novel, is stopped in his car by a policeman, he
feels that his "immunity" is over.

But to return to Italian literature, and to a related
theme, the critic Giacomo Debenedetti deals with Piran-
dello (and Federigo Tozzi) to illustrate what he calls "the
victorious invasion of the ugly ones": "a repertoire of rep-
resentatives of the squalid, the unpleasant, the sullen, the
dreary, the muddle-headed, the repulsive"; he explains
the origin of such a physiognomic or iconographic defor-
mation with Cézanne and expressionism. And, in tracing
the latest developments of the French nouveau roman, he
also proposes a collection of "anticharacters" with their
"predicates" and "ways of being" which include isolation,
extravagant dialogues, deprived and atonic existence, in-
communicability, insignificance, and inauthenticity.[14] If we
want to sum up the decline of the hero in one paradig-
matic example, we have passed from Odysseus, Homer's
Greek and epic hero, to Ulysses, Joyce's novelistic hero
from Dublin who (not by chance) follows *A Portrait of the
Artist as a Young Man*, which in turn is the forerunner of a
whole series of deformations on the same theme, the most
significant of which, in this context, is perhaps the *Portrait
of the Artist as a Young Dog* by Dylan Thomas (1941).

It seems therefore preferable to do away entirely with
the term "hero" and to use its opposite, "antihero," as Dos-
toevsky did, paradigmatically, for his "man from the un-
derground" who gathers within himself precisely and "de-
liberately all the characteristics of the antihero":
resentment, contemplative attitude, abjection, sense of

degradation to an insect or a mouse (almost a genetic met-
aphor of Kafka's Gregor Samsa), sense of guilt, neurosis,
inertia, revolt, the grotesque. . . . And all of these negative
characteristics of the antihero are literally (for the first
time, I believe) juxtaposed to those of "the hero of the
novel"; whereby, if we take into account the date of Dos-
toevsky's text, 1864, we cannot disagree with Trilling who
called the man from the underground "the eponymous
ancestor of a now numerous tribe."[15] The term "antihero,"
then, from the underground of a Russian and universal
soul, contains a reference to a human and literary past
perhaps lost forever, as well as to a problematic present, to
"this age of unadaptability, run through by philosophies of
anguish, an age which has arrived at the point of fetishiz-
ing its own malaise in that monstrous idol which is the
atom bomb, of conceiving projects for the end of the
world."[16]

Could we use a term like "strategy" in connection with
"antihero"? At first sight, such a metaphoric use might
seem a paradox, a contradiction in terms, if not an oxy-
moron—at least to the extent to which the antihero is the
exact opposite of the hero, who is the traditional referent
for such a soldierly concept as strategy. One needs only to
think of Napoleon, hero and strategist par excellence, the
model for a whole generation of romantic poets as well as
neoclassical artists, and the focus of the philosophic debate
in Hegel (philosophy versus history, or word versus
power). However, such a model is no longer valuable for
contemporary writers, who subject it to a true *diminutio an-
tiaulica*, as does Svevo for example in *Confessions of Zeno*,
with his ironic couplings of life and career and history and
nature, which are placed, moreover, at the beginning of a
chapter devoted to the antiheroic topic of "The Story of
My Marriage":

> In the minds of middle-class young men life is associ-
> ated with a career, and in early youth that career is

usually Napoleon's. They do not of course necessarily dream of becoming Emperor, because it is possible to be like Napoleon while remaining far, far below him. Similarly, the most intense life is summarized in the most rudimentary of sounds, that of a sea-wave, which from the moment it is born until it expires is in a state of continual change. I too, like Napoleon and like the wave, could at any rate look forward to a recurring state of birth and dissolution.[17]

It seems then that the metaphor used in the title of this chapter is necessary. When applied to the hero, "strategy" has an active, aggressive connotation; when applied to the antihero, it has a passive, self-defensive, self-ironic quality which, by itself, might suffice to characterize a historical shift manifested and documented particularly in and by the contemporary novel—although the simple mention of such works as Jaroslav Hašek's *The Good Soldier Schweik* (also taken up by Bertold Brecht), Ford Madox Ford's *The Good Soldier*, or Norman Mailer's *The Armies of the Night* (just to remain within a very specific semantic area) would suffice to enlarge the scope of the problem greatly.

In any case strategy points to the environment, not only to the subject, and this environment is definitely hostile, if not cruel and violent. If he wants to survive, the antihero must have a strategy of his own; he must somehow use the weapons provided by the environment for his own ends. Suffice it to think of the picaro, who is both active and passive, a fundamental figure in the development of the novel precisely in the sense indicated by Bakhtin, in that the picaro is strictly related to the notions of travel and transgression. Besides, the antihero, too, contains within himself certain elements of violence that are not too far removed from the notion and the practice of strategy (for instance it has been possible to talk about libertine or sadomasochistic strategies).

But above all, since the antihero, exactly like the hero, is simply a character, he cannot be anything other than part of the "strategy" of the author—a point that must be always kept in mind, especially in the case of the contemporary novel and its literary as well as cognitive contributions. Benjamin says that the critic is a strategist in the literary struggle: so is the author, obviously; and this struggle involves the reader, too, with his active perceptions and responses. If the environment is hostile and violent, the subject finds himself in a rapport of disharmony with it, a rapport for which contemporary sociology and literary criticism have a common, although not always precise, definition: alienation. I realize that to use the term "alienation" might cause some immediate reaction of annoyance or rejection, because this term has been perhaps excessively used and might give an impression of déjà vu. But putting the finger on the wound can be healthy. So, the alienated man can be considered the twentieth-century man par excellence, and as such he plays a central role in literature: he becomes the antihero, he is a member of an indeed numerous tribe. He is now ironic as in Robert Musil's *Man Without Qualities*; now intellectually rebellious, as in Sartre's *Nausea*; now indifferent, as in Moravia's *Time of Indifference* or in Camus' *The Stranger*; now angry, as in Döblin's *Berlin Alexanderplatz* (later brought to grotesque and resounding results by Grass' *The Tin Drum*); now deliberately abject, as in Céline's *Voyage to the End of Night*; now extremely learned and self-destructive, as in Canetti's *Auto da Fé*; now innocent and picaro at the same time, as in Salinger's *The Catcher in the Rye* or in Bellow's *The Adventures of Augie March*; now tormented, as in Borgese's *Rubè* or in Gadda's *Acquainted with Grief*; now not even existing, as for instance Agilulfo and Qfwfq in two books by Calvino, *The Non-existent Knight* and *Cosmicomics*—not to mention many other variations on the theme.

Perhaps the roots of contemporary alienation are to be traced (if one does not want to go back to Christian theology or Roman law) in the romantic attitude of the "fallen angel" in a debased, unworthy world, an attitude that found its philosophical expression in Hegel's phenomenology and a recent formulation in Morse Peckham's notion of "negative romanticism."[18] It is mainly psychological and ontological. But there is little doubt that the contemporary meaning of alienation derives directly from Marx and his description of capitalist society, where all human relations, within a class or between classes, become dehumanized, and the notions of reification and fetishism of commodities acquire a predominant role (in this connection, Lukàcs' *History and Class Consciousness* of 1923 is particularly eloquent).[19]

These notions become even more meaningful, more universal if possible, in Georg Simmel's sociological and philosophical conception: he considers them the inevitable result of human culture, as obeying a logic that is no longer that of the original spirit or subject but is inherent, intrinsically necessary to the cultural phenomenon itself: this is "the tragedy of culture," which cannot but alienate the citified, technological, modern man from his naturalness.[20] Only art is somewhat capable of achieving all the potentialities of the individual, but (here Simmel inspired Wilhelm Worringer directly) art reflects the sociocultural conditions from which it is born: expressions of naturalistic art correspond to periods of harmony between man and the cosmos, and expressions of abstract art correspond to periods of disharmony.[21] Such a distinction remains valid for contemporary art and literature, and its precise critical reflection can be seen in Joseph Frank's *The Widening Gyre*.[22]

Alienation in the Marxian sense should be juxtaposed to anomie, the concept developed by Durkheim, the positivists, and the behaviorists, for whom man is incapable of adapting himself to the changing conditions of society and should be so adapted by society itself, through "social engineering" or even, today, through psychoanalysis (obviously, I am not speaking of forced consent in totalitarian societies). Both Marxian alienation and anomie are very important for understanding the contemporary existential situation:[23] in fact they are those "abstractions" with which sociology deals in outlining "the dilemmas of modernity" and in criticizing its potentially negative developments.[24]

In such a context, there is no doubt that alienation in its various forms has enormous relevance for contemporary literature: it is, in fact, a "prime theme" as well as an underlying structure. But, as an English Marxist critic suggests, there is also another kind of alienation (*Verfremdung*): it is "a philosophy and technique of literature, particularly drama, primarily associated with Brecht and involving detachment, non empathy and disillusion. Art recognizing itself as art. Alienated art."[25] I think it legitimate to relate this artistic alienation to the "estrangement" (*ostranenje*) of the Russian formalist school: the two notions certainly do not coincide entirely, but they are undoubtedly similar and complementary; both are effective, not to say indispensable, for understanding contemporary culture. Moreover, both alienation and estrangement can and perhaps should be connected, on a higher level, to forms of "self-irony of art," through which the artist can "transcend his condition [of a limited man in the world] not in reality, but intellectually and fantastically."[26] This self-irony goes back to romanticism, and has been recognized and studied in its diversified manifestations and connections especially in lyric poetry, where it plays a major role. I shall only quote a comment by Ezio Raimondi on Baudelaire, as particularly relevant to my own critical stance: "The fall, the alienation of the *homo duplex* is transferred onto nature; and through alienation, the theatricality of the doubling of the self is reproduced, sanctioning the irony of the mask, the need for the artificial, the pleasure of disguise, the exasperated taste for convention."[27] I shall also, and not by chance, quote a remark by Paul De Man, again on Baudelaire: "Irony is unrelieved *vertige*, dizziness to the point of madness. Sanity can exist only because we are willing to function within the conventions of duplicity and dissimulation, just as social language dissimulates the inherent violence of the actual relationships between human beings. Once this mask is shown to be a mask, the authentic being underneath appears necessarily as on the verge of madness."[28] If Baudelaire appears, then, more than ever, to be the poet and essayist of modernity (as Montale would say), it is necessary to focus our attention on contemporary Italian literature, where the major thrust toward a representation of the theme of alienation and at the same time toward an overcoming of it (precisely through the strategies of the antihero) has occurred mainly at the beginning of this century, in the twenties.

More specifically, there was a brief but intense period, during which three major works in both the novel and poetry appeared: Italo Svevo's *La coscienza di Zeno* (Confessions of Zeno, 1923), Luigi Pirandello's *Uno, nessuno e centomila* (One, none, and a hundred thousand, 1925), and Eugenio Montale's *Ossi di seppia* (1925; the second edition in 1928 included "Arsenio," written in 1926-27). In highlighting these works, I follow a suggestion by Debenedetti: "If the character 'man' of the modern novel is a stranger, he also shadows the character of the hermetic poet, his attitudes and behavior."[29] I also follow, and expand, an idea by Montale himself, who introduced Svevo's Zeno by repeatedly emphasizing his qualities as a "European man."[30] A few diachronic considerations are in order before proceeding to the synchronic analysis of these works.

With *La coscienza di Zeno* Svevo concluded his oeuvre, begun in 1892 with *Una vita* (A life) and continued in 1898 with *Senilità* (As a man grows older). It marked a significant turning point in the Italian novel—doubly significant, in fact, because it represented a new and powerful view of the world after the ones established mainly by Alessandro Manzoni and Giovanni Verga in the nineteenth century (thus being juxtaposed to D'Annunzio's), and because, given precisely its novelty and power, it introduced modernism in Italian literature in a manner comparable to

what Joyce did for the English and Proust for the
French.[31] It might be appropriately remembered that
Svevo's fame was first of all European rather than Italian,
thanks to Joyce's enthusiastic support, which led to the
presentation of Svevo by Valéry Larbaud and Benjamin
Crémieux in France, while Montale (acting on a suggestion
by Bobi Bazlen) introduced the Triestine writer to Italian
readers in early 1925. The "dialogic" relation between
Svevo and Montale was established at that time, and it is
not the least in the complex network of European cultural
references outlined so far, and a truly meaningful one for
the topic under examination. In fact, Svevo used to exhort
Montale to abandon poetry and take up "the more reason-
able way of expressing himself," that is, prose![32]

In that same year, 1925, Pirandello's *Uno, nessuno e cen-
tomila* represented the culmination of his creative activity
both as novelist and as playwright: it is the last novel he
wrote, after working on it sparingly for more than a dozen
years and developing some of its themes and ideas in the
theatre, notably in the two masterpieces *Sei personaggi in
cerca d'autore* (Six characters in search of an author) and
*Enrico IV* (Henry IV) of 1922. It brings to extreme conse-
quences the existential intuitions of *Il fu Mattia Pascal*
(1904) and the intentions about a poetics of "L'umorismo"
of 1908-1920; it foreshadows the further, irrationalistic
developments of his latest plays; it is, in short, a *summa* of
Pirandello's revolutionary contribution to contemporary
literature, both in the theatre (an almost obvious assertion
is that Brecht, Beckett, Ionesco, and other playwrights
would have been impossible without him), and in the novel
(his accomplishments here were for a rather long time ob-
fuscated by his extraordinary success on the stage, but are
now increasingly recognized as fundamental ones, along
with Svevo's—and Gadda's).[33]

Montale's *Ossi di seppia* plays an equally fundamental
role in the history of its author, of Italian poetry, and of
contemporary poetry in general. It is the first book pub-

lished by the young poet, and it establishes the basis for his subsequent works, notably *Le occasioni* (The occasions, 1939) and *La bufera e altro* (The storm and other poems, 1957), but also *Satura* (1971), *Diario del '71 e del '72, Quaderno di quattro anni* (Notebook for four years), and *Altri versi* (Other lines), all collected now in the critical edition *L'opera in versi*. *Ossi di seppia* breaks with the predominant Petrarchan and Dannunzian tradition of Italian poetry, and powerfully inserts the problems and the language of conscience and analytical reason into an area where sentiments or irrationality dominated—even in the poetry of the other two great figureheads, Umberto Saba and Giuseppe Ungaretti. It had an enormous impact on whole generations of readers, and can be—actually has been—linked in many respects with T. S. Eliot's *The Waste Land*, that other milestone of contemporary poetry. In other words, *Ossi di seppia* is a fundamental work not only for what it is and says, but for how it has been historically received and interpreted (for instance, its "stoicism" according to Calvino and Arcangeli, discussed in the previous chapter), and for the cultural model it expressed and transmitted.

Svevo, Pirandello, and Montale are particularly representative of a major development in Italian literature in the twenties, the period when, according to Debenedetti, contemporaneity begins:[34] they are the poets of the modern conscience. As such, their works are indispensable for understanding contemporary alienation through their respective antiheroes. Zeno, Moscarda, and Arsenio are three fundamental specimens of what Caute calls "alienated art":

> What artistic writing can do is to move with a special freedom, creating new spaces of awareness, associating and juxtaposing features of reality, of consciousness, of myth, of aspiration and of belief in patterns and structures which could not be justified by academic or

scientific criteria. Like philosophy, it has a special mission to operate in the empty space between the known and the unknown, the verifiable and the speculative. And, like philosophy again, it enjoys a special exploratory relationship with man's most extensively employed means of communication—language.[35]

Here Caute seems to use an approach that can be usefully linked with L. A. White's notion of "the science of culture" or "culturology," where the cognitive role of art in general and literature in particular is not only recognized but given a precise, scientific status, and where the process of symbolization is not subordinated to logic or other disciplines. It seems unneccessary to emphasize how independently close and similar such conceptions are to Bakhtin's dialogic notion of culture.

While Caute uses the science of culture for ideological (that is, Marxist) purposes, the Italian critic Renato Barilli uses it for historicistic and literary ends, that is, for presenting Svevo and Pirandello as the two great innovators and founders of the contemporary novel through "a narrative bent on collaborating in the total institution of a new culture" through the rhetorical (communicative) means of their art. Barilli uses a formula that is acceptable perhaps more because of its polemical thrust than because of its historicist exactness: it is a culture that basically tends "toward the category of being rather than toward that of having" and is founded on the idea of "project" and not of "mirroring."[36] Barilli excessively privileges the notion of novelty, since in it everything appears to be positive, without reservations, while the "profound anguish of modernity" is well known, both in sociology (Peter Berger) and in literature (Debenedetti).[37] Barilli has the merit of having vigorously proposed the Svevo-Pirandello line, victorious over others, less powerful or successful in the Italian novel of the early twentieth century, and of having persuasively shown that the project of the two writers consists of indicating the possibility of a new and better mankind—and we might add that their "project" is situated precisely "in the empty space between the known and the unknown, the verifiable and the speculative."

Similar conclusions, of course, can be applied to Montale's poetry as well, and particularly to his early books. But it is important to stress that the specific end of my critical analysis is the discovery of structural similarities among different characters and works, the perception of their emblematic value, and the exploration of their status as literary devices. In other words, the context here is that of a thematic, symbolic criticism (Zeno, Moscarda, and Arsenio are considered as fundamental specimens of the antihero), and this criticism is broadened intertextually to explore the cultural meaning of the theme under examination (antihero as code and message) and the semiotic functioning of texts (along the communication axis going from the author-sender to the reader-addressee, without forgetting the context and the contact). For such a purpose I have prepared identity cards for the three characters: they contain precious elements which reveal their strategies, as well as those of their authors. A brief analysis of some of these significant elements will follow.

## 2. Zeno Cosini and Vitangelo Moscarda

Even in Zeno Cosini's name, as Renata Minerbi Treitel has shown, there is a hint to the concept of alienation: Zeno means "stranger," Cosini seems to point to "meaningless little things," and therefore to an acknowledgment and criticism of "reification" in Marxian terms.[38] But the really important aspect of this character (like Valéry's Monsieur Teste) is his "coscienza," his moral and psychoanalytic "conscience," his temporal "awareness," his totalizing "knowledge" or literary "con-science"—which is shown to be impossible. In other words, the emphasis is placed on interiority and contemplation rather than on behavior or action; individual values are placed above social ones. Zeno is a bourgeois, but a bourgeois picaro who does not really accept the social order around him, the one where he belongs historically: he does not work, has no financial preoccupations, and therefore can devote his time to the whims of his contemplative nature. To use the figure Benjamin pointed out in Baudelaire's poetry, Zeno is a flaneur, in the Triestine streets swept by the wind. He is perplexed, undecided, awkward to the point of being almost "Chaplinesque" (as some critics have defined him),[39] seemingly incapable of action, a "diseased" person perpetually searching for "health" but secretly glad and even proud of his sick condition, which privileges him above the "normal" state of the others. His awkwardness and illness are the surest signs of a wholly distorted, limping, deformed universe, subjected to chance and not to dialectics: man is alienated because he is not natural. Zeno is the very effective expression of a grotesque which is first and foremost metaphysical rather than historical or sociological.[40]

In narrative terms, Zeno's alienation is shown and superseded through characteristic thematic devices:

[1] Smoking the last cigarette, which is the brilliant lack of solution to a chain of insoluble dichotomies: between thought and life, will and thought, and—especially important for Svevo and the modern novel in general—chronological time and inner *durée*:

> I am sure a cigarette has a more poignant flavor when it is the last. The others have their own special taste too, peculiar to them, but it is less poignant. The last has an aroma all its own, bestowed by a sense of victory over oneself and the sure hope of health and strength in the immediate future. The others are important too, as an assertion of one's own freedom, and when one lights them one still has a vision of that future of health and beauty, though it has moved a little farther off.

The dates on my walls displayed every variety of
color and I had painted some of them in oils. The lat-
est resolution, renewed in the most ingenuous good
faith, found appropriate expression in the violence of
its colors, which aimed at making those of the preced-
ing one pale before it. I had a partiality for certain
dates because their figures went well together. I re-
member one of last century which seemed as if it must
be the final monument to my vice: "Ninth day of the
ninth month, in the year 1899." Surely a most signifi-
cant date! The new century furnished me with other
dates equally harmonious, though in a different way.
"First day of the first month in the year 1901." Even
today I feel that if only that date could repeat itself I
should be able to begin a new life.[41]

The long quotation is necessary to show the "logical"
connection between smoking a perpetually "last" cigarette
and the psychological mechanism of the resolutions to quit
smoking, and between these resolutions and the dates of
the calendar. But we should also note the extreme ele-
gance of Svevo's ironic wink at Dante, from the encounter
with Beatrice to the beginning of the *Vita nuova*, in a com-
binatorial game in which the dates of the calendar, of
chronological time, become pure pretexts for the inner,
existential *durée*.

[2] The death of the father, which not only is a perfect
example of the psychoanalytic ambivalence underlying the
most "normal" sentiments, but also establishes Zeno as nar-
rator, with an almost obvious reference, for today's reader,
to the "parricide word" that is placed by Derrida at the
very origin of any writing:[42]

My bitterest tears were shed on that sofa. Tears throw
a veil over our faults and allow us to accuse Fate with-
out fear of contradiction. I wept because I was losing
my father for whom I had always lived. It did not mat-
ter that I had been so little with him. Had not all my

efforts to become better been made in order to give satisfaction to him? It is true that the success I strove for would have been a personal triumph for me as against him who had always doubted me, but it would have been a consolation to him as well. And now he could wait no longer and was going away convinced of my incurable incapacity. The tears I shed were indeed bitter.

While I sit writing, or rather engraving these tragic memories on my paper, I realize that the image that obsessed me at the first attempt to look into my past— the image of an engine drawing a string of coaches up a hill—came to me for the first time while I lay on the sofa listening to my father's breathing. (p. 41)

The primary image, the matrix of Zeno's writing is then, without any possibility of doubt, the death of his father.

[3] His relationship with his wife Augusta, who is the perfect embodiment of the bourgeoisie, and with his lover Carla, who is romantic and possessive: both of them are necessary to establish Zeno's own detachment, diversity, and finally superiority:

"What made you give yourself to me? What have I done to deserve it?" [Zeno asks Carla].

"I thought it was you who had taken me," she said, smiling affectionately at me to show that she did not mean it as a reproach.

I remembered that women always insist on the fiction that they have been raped. But she soon saw she had made a mistake, for you may take things, but people must give themselves. . . .

As I lay there beside her, my love for Augusta revived in all its force. I had only one wish now: to hurry home to my wife, just in order to see her working like a busy bee, putting all our clothes away in camphor and naphthaline. (p. 190)

If Carla is, however mistakenly, "taken," and if Augusta is seen as a busy bee, Zeno, the one who takes and sees, is yet the one who above all judges.

[4] The story of his commercial association, which is a delightful mockery of the capitalist system from within, beginning with the commercial letters thrown up in the air and left to the chance of falling one way or the other in order to be answered or not, and ending with the buying and selling of a completely unmystical (that is, literally demystified) incense, a merchandise like any other—a perfect instance of a "gratuitous act."[43]

[5] The use of psychoanalysis as a means of narrating a story and of diversifying Zeno from the others, with the implicit but clear criticism both of the society made up of these others, and of psychoanalysis intended purely as a therapy: "disease" becomes a highly metaphoric term and, contrary to common expectations, acquires a positive value:

> Of course I have pains from time to time, but what do they matter when my health is perfect? I may have to put on a poultice now and then for some local ailment, but otherwise I force my limbs to keep in healthy motion and never allow them to sink into inertia. Pain and love—the whole of life, in short—cannot be looked on as a disease just because they make us suffer. . . .
>
> I am not so naive as to blame the doctor for regarding life itself as a manifestation of disease. Life is a little like disease, with its crises and its periods of quiescence, its daily improvements and setbacks. But unlike other diseases life is always mortal. It admits of no cure. It would be like trying to stop up the holes in our body, thinking them to be wounds. We should die of suffocation almost before we were cured. (pp. 396-97)

[6] The final apocalypse, which can be read as a "pharmakon," in the form of a warning, if not a prophecy, significantly directed against contemporary military strate-

gists: an enormous explosion caused by some sort of "Doomsday Machines" will free the earth from "parasites and disease," sweep it clean, and make it ready, perhaps, for a better and healthier mankind, or otherwise this same explosion will destroy the earth completely, returning it "to its nebulous state" (p. 397). Instead of quoting Svevo's page, which is famous anyway, I prefer to enlist the support of a well-balanced critical commentary by Sandro Maxia:

> In his radical nihilism he [Zeno] foresees the invention of an implement ["ordigno"] never seen before, a sort of Total Prosthesis which will save us once and for all from the fear of individual illness and death, even at the cost of cosmic death. But it is also possible—an interpretation of this type was proposed, and the text, in its profound ambiguity, seems to warrant it—it is also possible that the huge redeeming explosion alludes to the birth of a renewed world, the world of possibility (whose needs and exigencies no one can foresee now), for which the inept, the sketch-like Zeno has kept himself available, unlike the so-called healthy ones.[44]

Whatever the interpretation, in any case, a conclusion is sure: the enormous explosion that no one will hear ("Not with a bang but a whimper," Eliot would say) stands concretely and symbolically to signify that the universe is not anthropocentric, and such a conclusion is posited at the end of a novel that shows all the fragmentations, the "myriads of corpuscles" of an individual self and its "conscience."[45]

Stylistically, Svevo's literary strategy of the antihero is achieved especially through the following devices:

(a) The interposing of a note by a "Dr. S." between Zeno's diary, the author, and the reader, thereby providing an ideal distance to and from them and making the narrator a highly unreliable one, whose words can never be taken at face value and require an active deciphering by the reader: "He seemed to feel intense curiosity about himself," says Dr. S., the "editor" of the text, referring to Zeno: "But he little knows what surprises lie in wait for him, if someone were to set about analyzing the mass of truths and falsehoods which he has collected here" (p. 5). But of course, also the editor's voice is in turn ambiguous, ambivalent, problematic—certainly it is not an "authority" (and least of all an "authorial" one) that the reader can trust.

(b) The choice of a plain, "business" Italian, which is very discursive and nonpoetical, but highly communicative and therefore "didactic"[46]—the perfect linguistic instrument needed to illustrate the author's project, his world view.

(c) The narrator's awareness that he is telling simply a story, not the truth—in other words, the self-awareness of art recognizing itself as art and positing the necessity of its being art (in this case a novel rather than a sociological or medical treatise).

But let us turn now to Vitangelo Moscarda.

There is no particular meaning in the name of the protagonist and narrator of Pirandello's novel (unless there is a possible grotesque play on assonances and associations, for example an angel of life who likes "mostarda" or who, being irritable, "gli salta la mosca al naso," as the Italian saying goes, a fly jumps to his nose); but it is fair that it be so, because like his predecessor, Mattia Pascal, he is only a name to which one, none, and one hundred thousand entities correspond. His individuality is completely lost in the dehumanized relations of his society, yet this dehumanization is necessary for his highest self-awareness. Like

Zeno, Moscarda is a bourgeois who does not accept the bourgeois order at all. He, too, does not work and has no financial preoccupations, so that his contemplative nature can come to the fore from the very beginning. He, too, is often perplexed and undecided, seemingly incapable of action, awkward, a "madman" juxtaposed to the "sane" others and finally emerging above them. When he does decide and does act, his decision and action will be "gratuitous," scandalous, and revolutionary.

In narrative terms, Moscarda's alienation is shown through thematic devices that closely parallel the ones used by Svevo for Zeno, and that perform an analogous function in the structure of the novel:

[1] Looking at himself in the mirror, which (like Schlemihl's shadow) is the very image of the doubling of the self, of the chain of dichotomies between contemplation and action, thought and life, will and thought, self and other, and madness and sanity[47]; it might be worth remembering that the mirror-image has become almost a topos of contemporary art, from the novel (for example, Clappique in Malraux' *Man's Fate* or Roquentin in Sartre's *Nausea*) to painting (for example, Picasso's *Young Girl at the Mirror*). Here is Pirandello's version:

> But all of a sudden, as my thoughts ran like that, something happened to change my stupor to a looming terror. I beheld in front of my eyes, through no will of my own, the apathetically astonished face of that poor mortified body piteously decomposing, the nose curling up, the eyes turning over inward, the lips contracting upward, and the brows drawing together as if for weeping—they remained like that, in suspense for an instant, and then without warning came crumbling down, to the explosive accompaniment of a couple of sneezes. The thing had happened of itself, at a draught of air from some place or other, without that

poor mortified body's having said a word to me, and quite beyond any will of my own.

"To your health!" I cried.

And I beheld in the mirror my first madman's smile. (pp. 39-40)[48]

It should be noted that this text is entirely based on the grotesque, both thematic (the grimace) and stylistic: the truly dissonant sounds of "apatica attonita" (apathetic astonished), then "arricciare arrovesciare contrarre aggrottar" (curling up, turning over inward, contracting upward, drawing together), and finally "crollar due volte a scatto per lo scoppio d'una coppia di sternuti" (crumbling down, to the explosive accompaniment of a couple of sneezes)—all these sounds produce an unusual accumulation of double consonants which seem the explicit mirroring of the signified in the signifiers.

[2] The absence of the father (Moscarda is an orphan), with affective "ambivalence" and with "parricide words" that are even stronger—and certainly more dramatic, more theatrical—than Zeno's own:

Yet our birth was an involuntary thing in the life of that stranger, the indication of a deed, fruit of an act, something in short that actually causes us shame, arousing in us scorn and almost hatred. And if it is not properly speaking hatred, there is a certain sharp contempt that we are now conscious of in our father's eyes also, which at this second happen to meet our own. We to him, as we stand upright on our feet here, with a pair of hostile eyes, are something that he did not expect from the satisfaction of a momentary need or pleasure, a seed that he unknowingly cast, a seed standing upright now on two feet, with a pair of popping snail's eyes that stealthily survey him and judge him and prevent him now from being wholly what he would like to be, free, *another man* even with respect to us. (pp. 96-97)

[3] The relationship with his wife Dida, a very concrete and nasty embodiment of the bourgeoisie, and with the lover Anna Maria, romantic and possessive, both necessary to define his "nonidentity" (he is Gengè for the former and Vitangelo for the latter), and therefore to establish his final detachment and superiority—exactly as was the case with Zeno, but with an element of misogyny (autobiographical as well as cultural misogyny) which may point to a direct influence on Pirandello of Weininger's theories on the superiority of the male, considered as the carrier of spiritual values, over the female.[49]

[4] The story of his disengagement from his father's bank, which is a complete, literal rejection of one of the key institutions of capitalist society.

[5] The use of madness as a means of distinguishing Moscarda from the others, in order to criticize the system of social roles and the related bourgeois values attached to them. Witness the scene when Moscarda tells the two bankers, who believe him to be mad, to kneel in front of madmen: "Then go—go there where you keep those people locked up; go, go and listen to them talk! You keep them locked up because it's more convenient for you" (p. 150).

[6] The final, private, "pantheistic" dispersion into nature of the character, who has given up all his belongings, his social position, even his name—a dispersion which has the same function as Zeno's public apocalypse—that is, to point to the possibility of another, better world, different from the present one and projected into a hypothetical future.

Stylistically, Pirandello's literary strategy is achieved—significantly in a novel which is the epitome of his theatre—through the following devices:

(a) The fragmentation of the story into short chapters, much à la Tristram Shandy:[50] these short chapters are self-enclosed scenes doing away with the traditional plot and breaking the "story" continuously, showing it to be precisely that, a story.

(b) The choice of a middle Italian idiom, highly communicative and didactic, furthering a cognitive operation.

(c) The rhetorical addresses of the narrator, a "man from the underground," to the readers, such as the following, immediately underscored by a metatextual commentary in parentheses: "Was I not, in all truth, setting out to play a dirty trick upon Signor Vitangelo Moscarda? Yes, good people, that is what it was! a dirty trick (you will have to excuse all these winks on my part, but I have need of winking, to wink like this, since, not being aware just what impression I am making upon you at this moment, I may be able thus to obtain a hint)" (p. 131). These rhetorical addresses encourage, if not postulate, an "active, personal response,"[51] and provide space for it within the fiction itself: again, the self-awareness of art as such.[52]

## 3. Arsenio

Let us turn now to Montale's Arsenio. First, the text of the poem, "the most appealing and newest lyric, if not the most perfect, of *Ossi*":[53]

> I turbini sollevano la polvere
> sui tetti, a mulinelli, e sugli spiazzi
> deserti, ove i cavalli incappucciati
> annusano la terra, fermi innanzi
> ai vetri luccicanti degli alberghi.
> Sul corso, in faccia al mare, tu discendi
> in questo giorno
> or piovorno ora acceso, in cui par scatti

a sconvolgerne l'ore
uguali, strette in trama, un ritornello
di castagnette.

È il segno d'un'altra orbita: tu seguilo.
Discendi all'orizzonte che sovrasta
una tromba di piombo, alta sui gorghi,
più d'essi vagabonda: salso nembo
vorticante, soffiato dal ribelle
elemento alle nubi; fa che il passo
su la ghiaia ti scricchioli e t'inciampi
il viluppo dell'alghe: quell'istante
è forse, molto atteso, che ti scampi
dal finire il tuo viaggio, anello d'una
catena, immoto andare, oh troppo noto
delirio, Arsenio, d'immobilità . . .

Ascolta tra i palmizi il getto tremulo
dei violini, spento quando rotola
il tuono con un fremer di lamiera percossa;
la tempesta è dolce quando
sgorga bianca la stella di Canicola
nel cielo azzurro e lunge par la sera
ch'è prossima: se il fulmine la incide
dirama come un albero prezioso
entro la luce che s'arrosa: e il timpano
degli tzigani è il rombo silenzioso.

Discendi in mezzo al buio che precipita
e muta il mezzogiorno in una notte
di globi accesi, dondolanti a riva,—
e fuori, dove un'ombra sola tiene
mare e cielo, dai gozzi sparsi palpita
l'acetilene—
        finché goccia trepido
il cielo, fuma il suolo che s'abbevera,
tutto d'accanto ti sciaborda, sbattono

le tende molli, un frùscio immenso rade
la terra, giù s'afflosciano stridendo
le lanterne di carta sulle strade.

Così sperso tra i vimini e le stuoie
grondanti, giunco tu che le radici
con sé trascina, viscide, non mai
svelte, tremi di vita e ti protendi
a un vuoto risonante di lamenti
soffocati, la tesa ti ringhiotte
dell'onda antica che ti volge; e ancora
tutto che ti riprende, strada portico
mura specchi ti figge in una sola
ghiacciata moltitudine di morti,
e se un gesto ti sfiora, una parola
ti cade accanto, quello è forse, Arsenio,
nell'ora che si scioglie, il cenno d'una
vita strozzata per te sorta, e il vento
la porta con la cenere degli astri.

The winds lift the dust
over the roofs, in whirls, and on the deserted
places where hooded horses
sniff the ground, standing in front
of the shining windows of the hotels.
On the boulevard facing the sea you descend
in this day
now rainy now lit, in which it seems that there sprints
to upset the equal hours,
tied in a weft, a refrain
of castanets.

It is the sign of another orbit: you, follow it.
Descend to the horizon that is overhung by
a laden whirl, high over the waves,
more vagabond than them: a salty spray
whirling, blown by the rebellious
element to the clouds; make your step

on the ground creak, and the tangle
of seaweed trip you: that instant
is perhaps, much awaited, that makes you escape
from finishing your voyage, link of a
chain, motionless going, oh too well known
delirium, Arsenio, of immobility . . .

Listen among the palm trees to the trembling spurt
of violins, put out when the thunder
rolls with a shaking of smitten plate;
the storm is sweet when
Sirius spouts white
in the azure sky and far away seems the evening
that is near: if the thunderbolt etches it,
it ramifies like a precious tree
in the light that becomes rose: and the timpano
of the tziganes is the silent roar.

Descend in the midst of the darkness that is falling
and changes midday into a night
of lit globes, swinging on the shore—
and outside, where an only shadow holds
sea and sky, from the scattered boats palpitates
the acetylene—
                    until the sky drops
timorous, the ground steams while being soaked,
everything near you swashes, the wet awnings
flap, an immense rustle grazes
the earth, down are flabby shrieking
the paper lanterns in the streets.

So, lost amid wickers and dripping
mats, you a reed dragging its
roots along, slippery, never
eradicated, you tremble with life and reach out
toward a void resounding with stifled
laments, the brim swallows you
of the ancient wave that turns you; and still

everything that takes you back, street arcade
walls mirrors fixes you in a single
iced multitude of dead,
and if a gesture grazes you, a word
falls next to you, that is perhaps, Arsenio,
in the hour that is melting, the signal of a
strangled life arisen for you, and the wind
carries it with the ash of the stars.

Even before examining the traits of the eponymous
character, especially in relation to those of Zeno and Mo-
scarda, we should briefly check the phonic and figurative
levels of the poem and emphasize the metonymic function
of linguistic repetition, at least as far as the developments
from "Corno inglese" are concerned, since "Corno in-
glese" does indeed precede, prepare, and foreshadow "Ar-
senio."[54]

Here is, then, the "mimetic presentation" of the strident
sound of "un ritornello / di castagnette" in internal rhyme
with "tetti" and "strette" and in dissonance with the pat-
tern of *or* sounds (a last, residual echo of "Corno in-
glese"?): these *or*s are numerous in the first stanza (c*or*so,
gi*or*no, *or* piov*or*no *or*a, l'*or*e, rit*or*nello) and throughout the
poem, with a renewed frequency in the last stanza (anc*or*a,
p*or*tico, m*or*ti, f*or*se, nell'*or*a, s*or*ta, p*or*ta).

Here are the sibilants and fricatives of the third stanza:
"tra i palmizi il getto tremulo / dei violini," "rotola / il tuono
con un fremer di lamiera / percossa," "e il timpano / degli
tzigani è il rombo silenzioso": these dissonant phonic val-
ues are taken up and echoed in the crescendo of "trepido,
sciaborda, frùscio, s'afflosciano stridendo," and "lanterne
di carta sulle strade" (the approaching of the storm) in the
fourth stanza, and "strozzata, sorta, astri" in the last. It
should be noted that, again as in "Corno inglese," this se-
ries contrasts-harmonizes with a parallel series of nasals,
dentals, and palatals carefully varied: dis*ce*ndi, orizz*on*te,
tr*omb*a, pi*omb*o, vagab*on*da, *n*e*mb*o, vortic*ante*, elem*ent*o, in-

ciampi, istante, scampi, spento, tempesta, entro, timpano, rombo, dondolanti, ombra, accanto, tende, stridendo, grondanti, protendi, risonante, lamenti, onda, antica, vento.

Above all, at the phonic-semantic level, there is a truly extraordinary insistence, dissonant *vis à vis* the average norm of Italian, on proparoxytones: from "turbini, sollevano, polvere" (all in the first line) to "annusano" (in internal rhyme with "sollevano") and "sconvolgerne" in the first stanza; "orbita, seguilo," and "scricchioli" in the second stanza; from "tremulo, rotola," and "Canicola" (in rhyme and quasi-rhyme) to "prossima, fulmine, albero," and "timpano" in the third stanza; from "precipita, palpita, trepido" (again in rhyme and quasi-rhyme) to "s'abbevera, sbattono," and "s'afflosciano" in the fourth; from "vimini, viscide," and "portico" to "moltitudine" and "cenere" in the last. It is an impressive list, both because of the numbers (twenty-six terms) and the lexical choices, a list which is a truly comic, spoken language anticipating at the level of signifiers the meaning of the poem and of the character.[55] Hence it is possible to state that in "Arsenio" the object ends up looking like the poetry expressing it, in a circular structure typical of iconicity.

As for the figurative level, certainly the reader must have perceived the descriptive effectiveness of the poem, even in my literal translation and without any critical suggestion. There is in the text an accumulation of realistic as well as disquieting details, from the "hooded horses" that in "deserted / places sniff the ground" to the series of nouns "the boulevard, the palm trees, the lit globes, the scattered boats, the wet awnings, the paper lanterns, the wickers and the dripping mats," culminating in the lightning, paratactic sequence "street arcade / walls mirrors." They are all details of the setting, and they are the background (the context) for the central description of the poem, the storm which had been just touched upon in "Corno inglese": the laden whirl, high on the waves, more vagabond than them, a "salty spray / whirling, blown by the rebellious element to the clouds." Or consider the scene when Sirius appears in the sky "and far away seems the evening / that is near: if the thunderbolt etches it, / it ramifies like a precious tree / in the light that becomes rose"; this scene prepares not only the crescendo of the storm itself (already underscored at the phonic level), but especially the final stanza with Arsenio's inner landscape: "a void resounding with stifled / laments," "a single / iced multitude of dead."

Such mental visions are correlated to the metaphoric images of the poetic voice, which were in turn prepared by the corresponding ones of the second stanza ("The sign of another orbit," "link of a chain," "delirium of immobility"): they culminate in the "signal of a strangled life," "and the wind carries it with the ash of the stars." All these metaphoric images are an integral and extremely significant part of Montale's poetic discourse, to which we should turn our attention as it goes beyond the imaginary (the figurative) and is shaped in rational articulations—the forms of meaning.

Let us take up our critical itinerary at this level, with Arsenio's identity card. The old-fashioned name has the austere meaning of "burnt," already noted in chapter 1, to which, following another etymology, we might add an ironic hint at virility, in juxtaposition to Eusebio, the author's favorite nickname. It would seem to recall another poetic character like Eliot's Prufrock, rather than novelistic characters like Zeno and Moscarda.[56] Yet the linking, if not the comparison, of Arsenio with Zeno and Moscarda seems not only advisable but necessary.[57] Arsenio's identity card cannot be as complete as those of the other two antiheroes, precisely because he is a lyric and not a novelistic character, and among poetry's referents birth certificates are certainly not primary. Montale himself stated, in reply to a question: "I would not know what to say about poetic characters, especially today when characters tend to disappear even from the novel. Arsenio and the Nestorian are projections of myself. In any case the character who appears in a poem will be much more synthetic than the character of a novel. However, within certain limits, even verse can narrate,"[58] as is demonstrated for example by Montale's favorite poet, Robert Browning, "a great narrator in verse,"[59] who was dear to those, like "Pound and company," who "in writing their lyrics did not resign themselves to the limitations of the lyric genre but dreamed of a poetry that should be lyric and epic, chronicle and novel, elegy and hymn, satire and invective."[60] Arsenio, then, is a character nevertheless, and a very emblematic one, as an embodiment of Montale's major themes and as a catalyzer of culture.[61]

Like Zeno and Moscarda, Arsenio is shown to have all the traits of a bourgeois character who, however, does not seem to accept the bourgeois order, or at least to fit into it properly. He is a flaneur on the elegant seashore of some Riviera resort (presumably), and it is fair to assume that he does not have serious financial preoccupations; the city is deserted, but the crowd is inscribed in every scene of the poem (like the Parisian crowd in Baudelaire), and it is the experience of the crowd, the shock caused by it (*Erfahrung*, not *Erlebnis*) that determines the relationship between Arsenio and the landscape on the one hand, and between Arsenio and himself on the other.[62] So, Montale's poetic double is alone, absorbed in his own thoughts, undecided, perplexed, seemingly incapable of action and awkward in his strolls through pebbles and seaweeds, precisely "Chaplinesque," like Zeno, that is, like him, an improbable bourgeois clown. Besides, perhaps like a character by Musil, he appears to be very "atmospheric," if not meteoropathic and "without qualities."[63]

In narrative terms, as far as a narrative can be extracted from a poem, Arsenio's alienation is portrayed or conveyed through the following images:

[1] The doubling poet-character: Arsenio is the apathetic addressee of the imperatives or exhortations uttered

by the poetic voice ("follow it, descend, listen . . ."), and his difficulty of living is expressed by the identification with the "giunco," the reed that drags its roots along and is lost among wickers and dripping mats. We cannot exclude that the relationship reed-wickers, in superseding another one between life and death, becomes also an ironic hint to Montale's stoicism—he is like a reed, not a rock.

[2] The waiting for a storm, for "another orbit," for something that will terminate his senseless wandering, something posited beyond his present condition of "equal hours, tied in a weft," something that should somehow be the decisive element in an unsatisfactory existential condition.

[3] The "delirium of immobility," which expresses a dramatic dichotomy between life and the absolute, between Arsenio's thoughts and life; it can be compared with Zeno's time, described by Montale himself as "stagnating, yet always moving,"[64] as well as with Moscarda's present tense—a series of snapshots. This delirium of immobility is counterpointed by equivalent images throughout *Ossi*, notably in "In limine" ("Se procedi t'imbatti / tu forse nel fantasma . . . ," if you proceed you run / perhaps into the phantasm . . .) and "Mediterraneo" ("Il tuo delirio sale agli astri ormai," your delirium goes up to the stars); and it is also connected to those other metaphysical images, "the sign of another orbit," the "link of a chain," which point to a whole series of Montalean "varchi" (passages), from "I limoni" to "Corno inglese" again, or from "Crisalide" to "La casa dei doganieri."

[4] The final cosmic image, significantly introduced by a hypothetical clause ("if a gesture grazes you . . ."): "that is perhaps the signal of a strangled life arisen for you, and the wind carries it with the ash of the stars." I shall not insist here, especially after the analysis of "Corno inglese," on the presence and function of this wind in "Arsenio," a wind that like Shelley's destroys and preserves, is violent and creative, personal and universal with its echoes of lay

religiosity and visionary quality. I shall simply remark that
the ending of "Ode to the West Wind" resounds in "Ar-
senio," in an unequivocal manner, as my italics show:[65]

> Drive my *dead thoughts* over *the universe*
> Like withered leaves to quicken a *new birth!*
> And, by the incantation of this verse,

> *Scatter*, as from an unextinguished hearth
> *Ashes and sparks, my words* among mankind!

And if Shelley's romantic impetuousness and optimism are
attenuated in Montale, perhaps because of Debussy's and
Mallarmé's intertextual mediation,[66] I wish to emphasize
that the vision of the "ash of the stars" carried by the wind,
with the related sense of death in Arsenio, is the culmina-
tion of his estrangement, of his isolation, of his alienation
from the world of the living; it is, at the same time, the
culmination of his potential as a poet (along with the ash
of the stars, the wind does carry "the signal of a strangled
life arisen for you"). Thus the final image reflects both his
inner conscience and the external macrocosm; themati-
cally as well as structurally it corresponds to Zeno's apoca-
lypse and to Moscarda's annulment in nature. The global,
cosmic sense of death common to our three great authors
makes them share a typically modern, cultural climate, one
which Bernstein feels in Mahler's Ninth Symphony, a "mu-
sical presentation of death itself, which paradoxically rean-
imates us every time we listen to it."[67]

Stylistically, Montale's literary strategy of the antihero,
or of the poet who does not want to be laureate, who pre-
fers his own *diminutio antiaulica*, is carried out through
four poetic devices which have become almost common-
place in contemporary poetry (according to Friedrich's still
fundamental analysis). First, the use of the oxymoron
(such as "immoto andare," motionless going, or "rombo si-
lenzioso," silent roar) as a sign of the contradictory nature,
absurdity, and vanity of the whole reality. Second, the use

of the insistent imperatives (with the related "tu" form), which mark the difficult relationship of the poetic character with the others and the world, while the indicative mode, by contrast, would be the sign of his harmony with them and with it.[68] It should also be noted that from another point of view both the imperative and the vocative are fundamental elements for the specificity of poetry, because, if it is true that it is necessary "to distinguish two forces in poetry, the narrative and the apostrophic," one opposed to the other, apostrophe triumphs in the lyric: "Apostrophe resists narrative because its *now* is not a moment in a temporal sequence, but the *now* of discourse, of writing," which creates itself as an event.[69] Third, the choice of "objective correlatives" to indicate inner states of conscience, as well as to portray the fragmentation of external reality, its loss of unity and of meaning. Montale warns, however, that he "was moved by instinct, not by a theory (Eliot's 'objective correlative,' I believe, did not exist yet in 1928 when "Arsenio" was published in *Criterion*)," and that his goal was to break down the "barrier between the inner and the exterior," which seemed to him "nonexistent even from a gnoseologic viewpoint."[70] And finally, the use of a "broken" poetic language (negativity, dissonance), corresponding to the break in society and the world today, and instituting the self-awareness of poetry as poetry, in sharp contrast with D'Annunzio's high poeticity.

Zeno, Moscarda, and Arsenio are three emblematic characters because they are antiheroes envisaged by their respective authors not simply as mirrors of a crisis (alienated consciences), but as projects of a different and better idea of man (conscious alienation). Through their structural homologies and affinities they carry a precise symbolic meaning, they constitute a literary code and message, and they form part of a literary and cognitive strategy common to Svevo, Pirandello, and Montale, as well as to the few, true innovators of contemporary European literature.

It might be said that Zeno's apocalypse, Moscarda's pantheistic epiphany, and Arsenio's cosmic storm are a sort of "dystopia" or anti-utopia, analogous to the political allegories of Zamyatin, Huxley, or Orwell, which Caute characterizes as "didactic because they are warnings as well as prophecies."[71] It seems significant that such a message should be conveyed through the strategies of individual figures like Zeno, Moscarda, and Arsenio: "Literature, as an act of *revolt*, is historically structured and attuned to represent the *individual* constituent in the parliament of collective culture. . . . The last individualist is born not only out of the logic of liberalism, but out of the very womb of the novel,"—and of poetry as well, for that matter. Both in the case of the novel and of poetry, in fact, "it is a question of a literary construction of dystopia recognizing and exploring by means of internal alienations its own nature as sign, symbol, and book."[72] You will recall the references I made to the "liminality" of Montale's poetry "on the edge," posited between the imaginary and the real just like Morandi's etchings: these references are fully confirmed, and radicalized, by the notion of dystopia.

The logical conclusion that can be drawn from the preceding analysis is that only on a superficial level do the strategies of the antihero lead to some sort of self-destruction; on the contrary, while conveying what Kermode called "the sense of an ending,"[73] while being an unequivocal expression of the "disintegration of the integrity that an individual had possessed in epic (and in tragedy)," they are at the same time "the necessary preparatory steps toward a new, more complex wholeness, on a higher level of human development."[74] Thus the novelization of literature brings about a renewed assertion of man, no longer with a capital M, no longer Hero at the center of the universe, but still man, who carries with him, lucidly or comically, one of his highest values—the written, victorious word.

# Epilogue:
# The Plainclothes Clown

Every classic, when it is vital, is to be questioned outside of
conservative interpretations, in order to be a stimulus, a term of
confrontation, which is all the more substantive the more it is
inserted in the spirit of its time.
EZIO RAIMONDI,  *Tecniche della critica letteraria*

It is now necessary to probe further into the cultural
meaning of Montale's poetry, by taking into consideration
that aspect of Arsenio which is most intimately tied to his
being a poetic, in fact a metapoetic character, an icon of
meanings inherent in his very form. There is no doubt
that Arsenio is a projection of the poet, not only or not so
much in an autobiographical sense, but as "the poetic con-
sciousness that brings the poem into being," so that (to
complete Rebecca West's beautiful insight) "the poem it-
self, like its marginal protagonist, remains on the thresh-
old, and its primary message is that of the dynamism of its
own emergence into form."[1]
As poetic consciousness, Arsenio appears to hold a
prominent position in Montale's entire oeuvre: he is a fun-
damental focus toward which a whole series of modes con-
verges—from dissonance to *diminutio antiaulica*, from lim-
inality to alienation, from stoicism to self-irony, from the
self-conscious double to the antihero's objectification. These
modes allow us to consider Arsenio as the metonymic ex-

108

pression of modernity, an Italian Monsieur Teste or Monsieur Croche, both text and witness of so much contemporary culture. I shall group these modes according to two lines: the identification between Arsenio and the poet, and the identification between the poet and the mountebank. Both these identifications should be considered as summarizing as well as symbolic, almost a transcendental autobiography of Eugenio Montale. Remembering his constant and declared admiration for Baudelaire, the poet of modernity, it is not difficult to single out in the latter (following the critical itinerary sagaciously indicated by Raimondi) a dandyism that seems to me to be at the origin of many cultural attitudes of Montale as well, beginning with the stoicism that was shown to be so important for readers like Calvino and Arcangeli: "And since it is impossible to be a dandy without being aware of it, dandyism implies a role and a mask, as precisely the Stoics used to teach: only, instead of magnanimity and harmony with the cosmos, there is the certitude of downgrading and degradation, so that the sterile hero of eccentric originality, as soon as he becomes the poet of himself, discovers that he is a pariah, a mime, a mountebank, the grotesque face of tragic clear-sightedness."[2]

We need only adapt this quotation to Montale, who, although he did not critically thematize the figure of the dandy (as Baudelaire did), deals with it in an eccentric place, a report from England, "Paradiso delle donne e degli snob" (Paradise of women and snobs), where he describes British dandyism in the following terms:

> It is probably the gesture with which an individual protests against the overwhelming force of a nature external to us and of a social milieu that conditions us; it is the sign of a disharmony, of a lack of conciliation with the world. It is a gesture which implies at the same time optimism, desperation, and faith in the individual destiny of man. . . . I don't know up to which

point this humanistic dandyism—which was also Ugo Foscolo's and Herman Melville's, two non-Britons— will be able to resist the shock investing Great Britain. What survives of it is the compassion of man for himself, self-irony, the taste for distinguishing oneself from the amorphous mass, desire to give a style to life.[3]

Montale's report is concluded with a significant sentence: "So much is enough, for those who love Europe and its cultural heritage, to find themselves perfectly at home in England."[4] So Montale declares his identification with the dandy in a profound and absolute manner. Since the dandy, when he becomes the poet of himself, discovers he is a mountebank, a clown, we should now turn back to Montale's poetry, particularly to his remake of Debussy's "Minstrels," and above all to the skillful intertextual allusions of "Arsenio."

Let us first examine the identification between the character Arsenio and the poet. We should immediately recall a Montalean statement of 1951:

Having felt ever since my birth a total disharmony with the surrounding reality, the subject matter of my inspiration could not be other than *that* disharmony. I am not denying that fascism firstly, and the war afterwards, and the civil war later still, made me unhappy. However, there existed in me reasons for unhappiness that went much beyond and farther than these phenomena. I think it is a case of lack of adjustment, a psychologic and moral maladjustment which is typical of all natures with an introspective background, that is, all poetic natures.[5]

What is remarkable is Montale's insistence on *disharmony*, on the lack of conciliation with the world, perceived as the situation of both the dandy and the poet, and as a justification, for both of them, for their desire to give *a style* to life. Again in 1975 Montale reiterated: "My subject was the malaise of life and also the vain effort to disassemble it to see how it is made."[6] Certainly, these self-comments by Montale do not modify the historical, cultural, and political interpretations treated in the preceding pages of this book: they simply vindicate the rights of poetry, or better still, the rights and also the limitations of the poet in his human intentions: "I lived my time with the minimum of cowardice that was possible for my feeble strengths," and "I soon thought, and still think, that art is the form of life of the one who truly does not live—a compensation or a substitute."[7] Such explicit statements are then taken up in later poems, like "Botta e risposta I" (Thrust and parry I), in which Arsenio concludes his answer to the first thrust by his interlocutor with these words:

> Ma ora
> tu sai tutto di me,
> della mia prigionia e del mio dopo;
> ora sai che non può nascere l'aquila
> dal topo.[8]

> But now
> you know everything about me,
> my captivity and my afterwards;
> now you know that an eagle cannot be born
> from a mouse.

Or let us read "Per finire" (As an ending):

> Non sono un Leopardi, lascio poco da ardere
> ed è già troppo vivere in percentuale.
> Vissi al cinque per cento, non aumentate
> la dose. Troppo spesso invece piove
> sul bagnato.[9]

> I am not a Leopardi, I leave little to burn
> and living in percentage is already too much.
> I lived at five percent, do not increase
> the dosage. Too often, instead, it rains
> on the wet.

I believe I am not increasing the dosage if I emphasize
the "burning," typical of Montale's poetry from the very
beginnings of "the heart" in "Minstrels," and if I quote also
from "L'eroismo" (Heroism), the 1975 poem that should
have been titled "L'eroe mancato" (The hero manqué):[10]

> Clizia mi suggeriva di ingaggiarmi
> tra i guerriglieri di Spagna e più di una volta mi sento
> morto a Guadalajara o superstite illustre
> che mal reggesi in piedi dopo anni di galera.
> Ma nulla di ciò avvenne. . . .
> Qualche cosa ricordo. Un prigioniero *mio*
> che aveva in tasca un Rilke e fummo amici
> per pochi istanti; e inutili fatiche
> e tonfi di bombarde e il fastidioso
> ticchettìo dei cecchini.
> Ben poco e anche inutile per lei
> che non amava le patrie e n'ebbe una per caso.[11]

> Clizia used to suggest that I enlist
> among the Spanish guerrillas and more than once I
>   feel
> dead at Guadalajara or a famous survivor
> who is hardly able to stand on his feet after years in
>   jail.
> But nothing like that happened. . . .
> Some things I do remember. A prisoner—*mine*—
> who had a Rilke in his pocket and we were friends
> for a few moments; and useless labors
> and thuds of bombards and the annoying
> ticking of snipers.
> Very little, and even useless for her
> who did not love fatherlands and had one of them by
>   chance.

Self-irony, for sure, but also profound and lasting seri-
ousness. Let us read, a posteriori, the letter the young
Montale sent to his sister Marianna, from Parma on No-
vember 8, 1917, on the eve of his experience of the same

war evoked at a distance of many years in the quoted lines from "L'eroismo": "I am a friend of the invisible, and I don't take into account anything but what makes itself felt and does not show itself; I do not believe and I cannot believe in anything we touch and see. I am, then, just an *anti-military*. Even when I write, doesn't it seem as if I were talking in a soft voice in order to let it be understood, in between syllables, a bit of what I am unable to tell even myself?"[12] It can really be said that in between Montale's syllables there is always, in his entire itinerary as a man and an artist, a highly civilized fidelity to a lived and self-conscious antiheroism which is in turn an integral and fundamental part of the figure of the poet as a clown or mountebank.

We should recall that in chapter 1, while analyzing "Minstrels," I make reference to the presence of the topos of the clown in music, painting, and poetry, verifying above all its presence within the antiheroism of modern art without insisting too much on its meaning. It is now necessary to deepen and articulate this meaning. In his beautiful book, *Portrait de l'artiste en saltimbanque*, Starobinski suggests that the ironic play of artists who define themselves as *saltimbanques*, from Flaubert to Jarry, from Henry Miller to Joyce, from Rouault to Picasso, has the symbolic value of "a mocking epiphany of art and the artist. A criticism of bourgeois honor is doubled by a self-criticism directed against the artistic vocation itself. We must recognize such an attitude as one of the characteristic components of 'modernity.'"[13] Starobinski explores the anthropological origins of the clown (or acrobat, mountebank, harlequin), and points out its "original link with the realm of death" (p. 130), a link which is in turn articulated into the two complementary attitudes of angelism (the clown as a figure of Christ) and of satanism (the clown as a figure of the devil). They are

the opposite and complementary directions taken by the desire to go beyond the world, and more exactly to introduce into this world the testimony of *a passion which came from elsewhere and sees an elsewhere.* As a scapegoat, the clown is expelled from the world, carries our sins and shames, crosses into death; through his crossing, he makes us pass into salvation. As a transgressing demon, the clown rises among us as an intruder come from the external darkness: perhaps he is the one who had been expelled in the beginning, the menace that cannot be forgotten or rejected for long. (p. 136)

The clown's passage into death is further explained by Rilke's fifth Duino elegy (perhaps one of the poems Montale found in the pocket of his Austrian prisoner during World War One, whereby they became friends for a few brief moments?): "In Rilke the world of the *saltimbanques* is symbolically posited between earth and sky, between life and death, . . . where everything is ordered around the secret of a *passage* toward the work of art and its accomplishment, which in turn is an allegorical but insufficient anticipation of another passage, which will insure the true achievement of love in death."[14] Starobinski concludes that indeed Rilke's poet-mountebank passes from the "pure insufficiency" (of the body, the world, life) into the "empty overabundance" (of art and death). In such a passage, art displays its whole epistemological and creative, disquieting and salvific function: "In a utilitarian world, intertwined by the closely knit network of significant relationships, in a practical universe, in which everything is assigned a function, a value for use or exchange, the entrance of the clown makes some *mesh in the net* break, and into the suffocating fullness of accepted meanings, he opens up a *passage* through which a *wind* of disquietude and *life will blow*" (p. 141, italics mine). Really, I do not have to insist on the "Montalean" references of Starobinski's quotation. In Montale the clown, the metaphoric clown in everyday clothes who *breaks some mesh in the suffocating net* of accepted

meanings and opens up *a passage, a way* through which a
*wind* of disquietude and *life will blow* is Arsenio, and Ar-
senio is the poet's double, as we know. (It might be worth
recalling in this context that for Montale poetry is "music
made with words and even with ideas.")[15]

Starobinski's statement is astonishing because it does not
appear that he had Montale in mind at all; whereby it can
be said that language claims for itself (at a cultural and an-
thropological level) those figures that animate the dis-
course (the *parole*) of both the critic and the poet: the met-
aphors of the broken mesh in the net, of the opening in
the accepted meanings, and of the wind of disquietude
and life are part of a general, human experience, they are
expressive clichés functioning as such in the critic's lan-
guage, as codes carrying meanings, while in the poet they
are first of all inserted into a syncategorematic chain, into
a metonymic context from which they derive their primary
force as signifiers (and only secondarily as signifieds, as
meanings). Then the active participation of the reader is
necessary, who must be able to link the two different texts
and make them interact. We are dealing then with figures
of a dialogic discourse, which is central to the novelization
of literature and is above all a lively testimony of the "Eu-
ropean man," the modern antihero.

In concluding, I propose a metonymic (and emblematic)
interpretation of Arsenio as a "portrait of the artist as a
*saltimbanque*" in Starobinski's sense. It is worth repeating
and grouping here again the textual elements on which
the possibility of this interpretation is based.

Accompanied by "a refrain of castanets," by "the trem-
bling spurt of violins," and by "the timpano of the tzi-
ganes" (instruments and musical forms played by minstrels
that would not be out of place in a circus), Arsenio appears
on the scene of the poem with a descending movement, "in
the midst of the darkness that falls": he is an ambivalent
figure, literally come from "the external darkness," symp-
tom of a passion that "sees an elsewhere," carrier of a mes-

sage of salvation and/or menace. He is "lost amid wickers and dripping mats," clumsy, a "reed" dragging its roots along, and at the same time he "tremble[s] with life and reach[es] out toward a void resounding with stifled laments"; like an acrobat in precarious balance in his "delirium of immobility," Arsenio is certainly suspended between life and death, between earth and sky, between the "pure insufficiency" of the real milieu around him ("street arcade walls mirrors") and the "empty overabundance" of his inner landscape ("a void resounding with stifled laments," "a single iced multitude of dead"). He is the alter ego whom the poet urges to follow "the sign of another orbit" which upsets "the equal hours, tied in a weft," to catch that much-awaited instant that should make him "escape from finishing [his] voyage, link of a chain, motionless going. . . ." Everything is ordered symbolically "around the secret of a *passage* toward the work of art and its accomplishment," which is in turn, as in Rilke, "an allegorical but insufficient anticipation of another passage"; when the storm is unleashed "in the hour that is melting" (that is, in the time of liminality), Arsenio remains definitely suspended between life ("a strangled life") and death ("the ash of the stars"), both of which are carried by the wind which blows through, which *is* Montale's poetry.

The substantial and formal essence of this poetry can be said to be the effort of a metaphysical mountebank to conjoin the extremes, to "receive the irrational into his spiritual world, but without renouncing reason."[16] It is then a "poetry of experience" in search of truth that cannot be univocal and definite because it is entangled in diverse languages: hence the importance (not only stylistic, but epistemological and dialogic) of dissonance and *diminutio antiaulica*. Hence the meaning of Montale's impossibility of reaching the absolute expression, and therefore the suspension of poetry between the real and the imaginary, its tension toward a virtual perfection that can be approached at best metonymically, but without ever giving up, always insisting firmly, stoically, in the effort. And this constantly renewed effort expresses the dynamism, the openness, the modernity of a poetic word, Montale's, that is among the most intense and self-possessed in the European culture of this century.

If we remember, with Raimondi, that from Baudelaire onward modernity shows itself "with its double face—daily and novelistic, ridiculous and sublime,"[17] we can certainly understand Montale's late but definitive "salvaging" of "Minstrels" into his oeuvre in verse; and I believe that the centrality of the figure conceived as his poetic double— dressed in the grey suit of the daily novelistic or, as he would put it, "in the epic of the grey causality of our everyday life"[18]—will stand out in all its emblematic clarity: Arsenio, the clumsy bourgeois antihero, the sublime and ridiculous mountebank, the Schlemihlian shadow which elsewhere in *Ossi di seppia* "la canicola stampa sopra uno scalcinato muro," the noonday sun imprints on an unplastered wall.

# Notes

## Chapter One. Debussy and the Wind

1. Eugenio Montale, *Sulla poesia* (Milan: Mondadori, 1976), p. 563. Vittorio Pica (1864–1930) was an influential art journalist and for many years the secretary of the Venice Biennale exhibitions. He was an avant-garde critic who discovered and promoted many movements and artists, in both literature and the visual arts. Besides the French impressionists, he emphasized the importance of the symbolists. Among his numerous collections of essays are *All'avanguardia, L'arte dell'Estremo Oriente*, and *L'arte europea*. It should be noted that Pica had another great merit: he was among the very first to write a critical presentation in Italy of Mallarmé's oeuvre, in an article of 1886 now in *Letteratura d'eccezione* (Milan: Baldini e Castoldi, 1889); see Olga Ragusa, *Mallarmé in Italy: A Study in Literary Influence and Critical Response* (Ph.D. diss., Columbia University, 1954), pp. 77ff.

2. On this subject one should see at least three books by Eugenio Montale: *Pastelli e disegni* (Milan: Scheiwiller, 1966); *Farfalla di Dinard* (Milan: Mondadori, 1960); and *Prime alla Scala* (Milan: Mondadori, 1982); as well as the biography by Giulio Nascimbeni, *Eugenio Montale* (Milan: Longanesi, 1969).

3. See especially Mikhail Bakhtin, *The Dialogic Imagination*, tr. C. Emerson and M. Holquist (Austin: University of Texas Press, 1980), and *Speech Genres and Other Late Essays*, tr. V. McGee, ed. C. Emerson and M. Holquist (Austin: University of Texas Press, 1986).

4. Suffice it to recall the many pages devoted by Hugo Frie-

drich to the structural unity among modern poetry, music, and painting in *The Structure of Modern Poetry*, tr. J. Neugroschel (Evanston, Ill.: Northwestern University Press, 1974); and Eugenio Montale, *Quaderno genovese*, ed. L. Barile (Milan: Mondadori, 1983), p. 41: "*Modern art*. It is a fact that literature tends more and more toward musicality and color, while music and painting are directed fully toward literature. This is a key to remember." It is to be noted that this entry is dated 1917.

   5. Félix Fénéon, *Au-delà de l'impressionisme*, ed. F. Cachin (Paris: Hermann, 1966), pp. 84–85; the text is from 1887. See also John Rewald, *The History of Impressionism and Post-Impressionism* and *Post-Impressionism: From Van Gogh to Gaugin* (New York: Museum of Modern Art, 1973 and 1978 respectively). These two volumes are fundamental to following the complex relationships among impressionists, post-impressionists and symbolists, relationships at the very base of the developments of modern painting, beginning with Paul Cézanne.

   6. See Walter Benjamin, "On Some Motifs in Baudelaire," in *Illuminations*, tr. H. Zohn, ed. H. Arendt, pp. 155–200 (New York: Schocken, 1969), p. 197 n. 8:

> The daily sight of a lively crowd may once have constituted a spectacle to which one's eyes had to adapt first. On the basis of this supposition, one may assume that once the eyes had mastered this task they welcomed opportunities to test their newly acquired faculties. This would mean that the technique of Impressionist painting, whereby the picture is garnered in a riot of dabs of color, would be a reflection of experiences with which the eyes of a big-city dweller have become familiar. A picture like Monet's "Cathedral of Chartres," which is like an ant-heap of stone, would be an illustration of this hypothesis.

See also Anne Higonnet, Margaret Higonnet, and Patrice Higonnet, "Façades: Walter Benjamin's Paris," *Critical Inquiry* 10, no. 3 (Mar. 1984), pp. 391–419.

   7. See Ardengo Soffici, *Scoperte e massacri: Scritti sull'arte, 1908–1913*, 2d ed. (Florence: Vallecchi, 1929), pp. 235, 209–93; and Fénéon, *Au-delà de l'impressionisme*, pp. 135–37.

   8. Vittorio Pica, *Gl'Impressionisti Francesi* (Bergamo: Istituto Italiano d'Arti Grafiche, 1908), pp. 55 and passim. The book has

252 illustrations and ten plates, and a long chapter on Monet, "the most convinced and most aware initiator of the movement, and the clearest, most trustworthy, and most complete representative of impressionism" (p. 51). Renoir is defined "a virtuoso of chromatic dissonances" (p. 98), and there is even doubt placed on the very label "impressionism," "a rather inaccurate name" (p. 14).

9. Laura Barile, in Eugenio Montale, "Tre articoli ritrovati," ed. L. Barile, *Inventario*, n.s., 4 (Jan.–Apr. 1982), pp. 11 and 20 n. 18. Renato Serra (1884–1915) was a writer, critic, and intellectual who might have countered Benedetto Croce's influence, had he not died in World War One. His most important work was "Esame di coscienza di un letterato" (on the relationship between literature and war), but all of his letters and his literary, moral, and political writings (*Scritti letterari, morali e politici*) are worth remembering. On Serra see the critical commentary by Gianfranco Contini, *Altri esercizi, 1942–1971* (Turin: Einaudi, 1978), pp. 77–100, and especially the fundamental pages by Ezio Raimondi, *Il lettore di provincia: Renato Serra* (Florence: Le Monnier, 1964). On Bastianelli and *La dissonanza* see Barile, in Montale, *Quaderno genovese*, p. 139.

10. Eugenio Montale, *Auto da fé* (Milan: Il Saggiatore, 1966), pp. 113, 111 (from a piece dated 1949), and 244 respectively. On this problem see the ample treatment by James Anderson Winn, *Unsuspected Eloquence: A History of the Relation Between Poetry and Music* (New Haven: Yale University Press, 1981).

11. Montale, *Sulla poesia*, p. 144.

12. Ibid., p. 565.

13. Leonard Bernstein, *The Unanswered Question* (Cambridge, Mass.: Harvard University Press, 1976).

14. Marzio Pieri, *Biografia della poesia* (Parma: Edizioni della Pilotta, 1980), p. 251: "How much Debussy in the young Montale!" Interestingly, in his *Storia della poesia italiana del Novecento* (Milan: Mursia, 1976), pp. 224–25, Silvio Ramat describes the structure of *Ossi di seppia* as "a harmonization" between the recitative of the short compositions and the "cantato" of "Mediterraneo."

15. Eugenio Montale, *L'opera in versi*, ed. G. Contini and R. Bettarini (Turin: Einaudi, 1981), p. 913, and *Quaderno genovese*, pp. 37–38: "Last Tuesday the excellent Malchiodi, who is

going to be a lieutenant in the artillery corps, came to visit me. He played three pieces by Debussy ("Minuet," "Jardins sous la pluie," and "En Bateau"). The first two are superlative, the third mediocre." Barile has interesting remarks on Montale's musical aspects. She notes that *Farfalla di Dinard* is filled with "cavatinas, F-sharps, B-flats, and tenor embroideries," and points out that the poet "frequently and explicitly mentions certain musical forms or phrases, such as farandole, fandango, fantasia, and motet," in Montale, "Tre articoli ritrovati," p. 10. Of course the list could be lengthened.

16. Montale, *Auto da fé*, p. 301, from "Per fortuna siamo in ritardo" of 1963. I do not necessarily agree with his limiting judgment about the "macchiaioli" painters.

17. Montale, *Sulla poesia*, p. 57.

18. Ibid., p. 265; see also pp. 266–67.

19. Also in *Prime alla Scala* (e.g., p. 265), Puccini is interpreted in a modern dimension, filled with possibilities and restlessness, in line with recent contributions such as Enzo Siciliano, *Puccini* (Milan: Longanesi, 1977); Mosco Carner, *Puccini: A Critical Biography* (New York: Holmes and Meier, 1977); and Mario Bortolotto, *Consacrazione della casa* (Milan: Adelphi, 1982), pp. 131–51.

20. See *Sulla poesia*, p. 603: "I believe that my poetry is the most 'musical' of my time (and even of earlier times). Much more than [Giovanni] Pascoli's and Gabriele [D'Annunzio]'s. I am not claiming I have done more and better than them. Music was added to D'Annunzio by Debussy."

21. Nicholas Ruwet, *Langage, musique, poésie* (Paris: Seuil, 1972), p. 44.

22. Guido Salvetti, *Il Novecento I*, vol. 9 of *Storia della Musica*, under the auspices of Società Italiana di Musicologia (Turin: EDT, 1977), p. 43. A notation by Montale should be emphasized, concerning those years and the developments of the "new music": "Having abolished the dominant, excluded thematization (which privileges certain notes above others), granted the principle that in a composition any note is always a beginning and an end, and that the center should be everywhere and nowhere, musicians teach poets, and the latter accept the lesson," in *Sulla poesia*, p. 239. For a fascinating portrait of Paris, the city that was in part Debussy's milieu, see Roger Shattuck, *The Banquet Years: The Arts in France, 1885–1918* (New York: Vintage, 1968), with its parallel

biographies of Henri Rousseau, Eric Satie, Alfred Jarry, and
Guillaume Apollinaire.

23. Bortolotto, *Consacrazione della casa*, p. 69. On the subject
see also the beautiful catalogue *Debussy e il simbolismo*, ed. G. Co-
geval and F. Lesure (Rome: Palombi, 1984), with its rich icono-
graphic and documentary materials.

24. Pierre Boulez, *Relevés d'apprenti* (Paris: Seuil, 1966), p. 346.

25. Robert P. Morgan, "Secret Languages: The Roots of Mu-
sical Modernism," *Critical Inquiry* 10, no. 3 (Mar. 1984), p. 443.

26. Bortolotto, *Consacrazione della casa*, p. 74, and Salvetti, *Il
Novecento I*, p. 45.

27. Boulez, *Relevés d'apprenti*, pp. 345–46.

28. Salvetti, *Il Novecento I*, p. 46. Massimo Mila agrees with this
critical categorization in *Breve storia della musica* (Turin: Einaudi,
1977), p. 358; Stefan Jarocinski, on the contrary, rejects the
terms "impressionism" (as mistaken) and "symbolism" (as insuffi-
cient), for a definition of the composer, in *Debussy: Impressionismo
e simbolismo*, Italian trans. (Fiesole: Discanto, 1980). Even Debussy
refused these terms, for instance in his *M. Croche, autodilettante*;
however, they maintain their cultural and historical usefulness,
which should not be neglected, especially in relation to the young
Montale—and the same is true of the concept of dissonance it-
self.

29. On the social and technical characteristics of Wagner's mu-
sic see the fundamental essay by Theodor Adorno, *In Search of
Wagner*, tr. R. Livingstone (London: NLB, 1981); for a broader
outlook see Alfred Einstein, *Music in the Romantic Era* (New York:
Norton, 1947).

30. Salvetti, *Il Novecento I*, p. 46. Boulez notes that "the epoch
when he lived compelled Debussy to find at times elusive, feline
solutions" (*Relevés d'apprenti*, p. 347), and it is significant that Bor-
tolotto, too, praises "the shrewdness, the catlike prudence" dis-
played by Debussy, who "smoothes the too harsh linkage of
notes" and produces a "harmonic softening" (*Consacrazione della
casa*, pp. 88–89). In any case, in musical historiography it is pre-
cisely the concept of the purity of sounds that is outlined as char-
acterizing Debussy. For instance, already Paul Claudel empha-
sizes impressionistically the "diaprure" in the music of "le Claude
national," in *Oeuvres complètes* (Paris: Gallimard, 1960), vol. 17,
*L'oeil écoute*, p. 150. In a more modern manner, Jarocinski insists

upon "the sound thought" entirely directed toward the liberation of the purity, not the nuance, of sounds (*Debussy*, passim). Piero Rattalino also notes that in Debussy "the timbres are not fused, but simply coexist, and the sense of a hierarchy of values between melody and accompaniment is lost in favor of a co-presence of numerous independent sounds," in *Storia del pianoforte* (Milan: Il Saggiatore, 1982), pp. 272–73.

31. Salvetti, *Il Novecento I*, pp. 46–47. See also Bernstein, *The Unanswered Question*, pp. 147–89, and Bortolotto, *Consacrazione della casa*, p. 89, who considers the leitmotivs in *Pélleas* "not structural as in Wagner, but psychological and atmospheric." Melody is the "organizing force" of Debussy and the "musical counterpart" to the winding line of Art Nouveau, according to Arthur Wenk, *Claude Debussy and the Poets* (Berkeley: University of California Press, 1976), pp. 180 and 186–87. On the same topic see also Ruwet, *Langage, musique, poésie*, pp. 70–99 ("Note sur les duplications dans l'oeuvre de Claude Debussy"), and Jarocinski, *Debussy*, pp. 157, 164, and 195.

32. Bernstein, *The Unanswered Question*, pp. 243–45, 249, and 259.

33. Respectively Salvetti, *Il Novecento I*, pp. 51 and 53, and Jacques Rivière, *Études* (Paris: Gallimard, 1944), pp. 131 and 133–34. For his part, Montale noted that Debussy was "a great musician above all when he discovered the piano on his own, with a prodigious immersion into the civilization of his country, from Rameau-Couperin to Monet and Renoir," in *Prime alla Scala*, p. 13.

34. Salvetti, *Il Novecento I*, p. 54: "Let us remember the titles: for five fingers, for the thirds, for the fourths, for the sixths, for the octaves, for eight fingers; for chromatic degrees, for the embellishments," and so on and so forth.

35. Jarocinski, *Debussy*, p. 193. Bortolotto, *Consacrazione della casa*, pp. 90–91, stresses a consonance between Debussy and Baudelaire.

36. Boulez, *Relevés d'apprenti*, p. 347.

37. Montale, *Prime alla Scala*, p. 239.

38. On this subject see Montale, "Tre articoli ritrovati," particularly his review of Georges Duhamel's and Charles Vidrac's *Notes sur la technique poétique*, pp. 5–6, where he is interested in the theory of "that subspecies of free verse called 'white verse': to

be clear, a verse concerned with the intrinsic rather than external musicality, with a greater adherence to the nuances of spiritual life, and with a certain pathetic aridity which would be capable, more than the *faux exprés* rhythm of the early symbolists, of suggesting the echoes and fancies of intelligence." We should note such expressions as "greater adherence," which will be taken up again in the imaginary interview of 1946 in a different context, or "aridity" and "intelligence," which are true self-definitions of Montale's poetry. See also Barile's comments, ibid., pp. 7–8, and in Montale, *Quaderno genovese*, p. 108 (the references are to Montale, *Sulla poesia*, pp. 111–17):

> The theme of the autonomy of aesthetic reality, connected with the two poles of decadentism, will be central in the development of Montale's poetry. On the one hand there are the lyric poets of "the pure intuitive flashes," the Coleridge of *Kubla Khan* and the Rimbaud of *Illuminations*—the line where Ungaretti belongs; and on the other hand there is a poetry which does not give up "the structural-rational cement" rejected by the former poets, but justifies it, in terms of poetic results, with the "deepening of musical values."

39. Montale, *Sulla poesia*, p. 58.

40. Ibid., p. 581. On the importance of Browning see at least the comments by Barile in Montale, "Tre articoli ritrovati," pp. 13–16. On Baudelaire's modernity see in particular Stanley Cavell, *The World Viewed: Reflections on the Ontology of Film* (New York: Viking, 1971), pp. 41–46, on Baudelaire and myths in film, pp. 47–55, on the figures of the military and the woman, and pp. 56–60, on the dandy. See also Ezio Raimondi, "Prefazione," in Charles Baudelaire, *Scritti sull'arte*, Italian trans. (Turin: Einaudi, 1982), p. xiv: "Among the constant themes recurring throughout Baudelaire's critical meditations like a wide spiral, . . . the sharpest and boldest idea is undoubtedly that of modernity." This essay is now reprinted, with the title "Il romanzo nelle figure," in his *Il volto nelle parole* (Bologna: Il Mulino, 1988), pp. 23–80.

Born in 1924, Raimondi studied at Bologna with Carlo Calcaterra and Roberto Longhi. Holder of the chair of Italian literature at the University of Bologna, he is perhaps the foremost contemporary Italian critic and certainly one of the most informed and open minds, interested in theoretical, methodological, historical, stylistic, and cultural issues and problems. Among his numerous critical works: *Tecniche della critica letteraria, Metafora e storia, Politica e commedia, Il silenzio della Gòrgone*, and *Il volto nelle parole*. His essay "Language and the Hermeneutic Adventure in Literature" appeared in *Forum Italicum* 18, no. 1 (Spring 1984), pp. 3–25.

41. Also according to Arnold Schönberg, the emancipation of dissonance as the elimination of the harmonic base is the foundation of dodecaphony: *Stile e idea*, Italian trans. (Milan: Rusconi e Paolazzi, 1960), pp. 109–10. What for Theodor Adorno, in his *Philosophy of Modern Music*, tr. Anne G. Mitchell and Wesley V. Blowster (New York: Seabury Press, 1973), is an insoluble contrast between Stravinsky and Schönberg, between tonal and atonal music, becomes more appropriately for Bernstein (in the last part of *The Unanswered Question*) a dialectic relationship indispensable for understanding the pathos and vitality of twentieth-century music.

42. The Italian critic and poet, Sergio Solmi, spoke of "the ground of radical modernity" in which the early poetry of Montale grew, "La poesia di Montale," in *Scrittori negli anni* (Milan: Il Saggiatore, 1963), p. 285. Solmi also suggests a line Heine-Laforgue-Govoni, to which Aldo Palazzeschi is added by Lanfranco Caretti in "Un inedito montaliano [Suonatina di pianoforte]," *Paragone* 336 (1978), p. 5.

43. Jarocinski, *Debussy*, p. 178. The importance of the sea and the comparison with Turner are also treated by Wenk, *Debussy and the Poets*, pp. 205–10, who quotes an interesting letter by Debussy, absolutely opposed to the term "impressionism" used by the "imbéciles" to define Turner, "le plus beau créateur de mystère qui soit en art."

44. Cf. Marco Forti, *Eugenio Montale* (Milan: Mursia, 1973); Edoardo Sanguineti, *Ideologia e linguaggio* (Milan: Feltrinelli, 1965); and Silvio Ramat, *Montale* (Florence: Vallecchi, 1965).

45. All the quotations refer to the critical edition of Montale, *L'opera in versi*, pp. 765–72.

46. Montale, *L'opera in versi*, p. 866; the text of the poem is on p. 14.

47. Montale, *Quaderno genovese*, pp. 33–34. Barile's comment (ibid., pp. 138–39) is worth quoting extensively: "The novelty of Debussy's music that most struck Montale at that time [1917] was

not so much his conception of harmony as a factor of expression valuable in itself; rather, it was his use of dissonance (the final 'white key, dissonant and jarring'), that is his refusal to resolve the dissonance in a subsequent consonance." A remark on p. 140 is also important: "Even if Debussy's music was the means through which Montale entered the core of decadent poetics and of the great themes of twentieth-century irrationalism, nevertheless it remains just a moment, which was soon superseded by the poet."

48. Massimo Mila, *L'esperienza musicale e l'estetica* (Turin: Einaudi, 1956), p. 180. Cf. Rattalino, *Storia del pianoforte*, pp. 324–25: among the great contemporary pianists, Gieseking was one of the first to include Debussy "constantly and frequently" in his repertoire.

49. Jarocinski, *Debussy*, p. 168.

50. Cf. Wenk, *Debussy and the Poets*, pp. 19–23.

51. An interesting connection in this cultural area is proposed by Dario Corno, "Petruška e Montale: Per una semiotica dei personaggi," *Strumenti critici* 39–40 (Oct. 1979), pp. 301–21.

52. Jean Starobinski, *Portrait de l'artiste en saltimbanque* (Geneve: Skira, 1970). On Aldo Palazzeschi see Fausto Curi, *Perdita d'aureola* (Turin: Einaudi, 1977); Guido Guglielmi, *L'udienza del poeta* (Turin: Einaudi, 1979), especially for the references to Starobinski, Baudelaire, and Freud (pp. 18–52 and 53–88); Piero Pieri, *Ritratto del saltimbanco da giovane: Palazzeschi, 1905–1914* (Bologna: Pàtron, 1980); and Mario Luzi, *Discorso naturale* (Milan: Garzanti, 1984), p. 22.

53. Silvio Ramat, *Protonovecento* (Milan: Il Saggiatore, 1978), p. 486; and Forti, *Montale*, p. 82.

54. Benjamin, "On Some Motifs in Baudelaire," pp. 155–56. Luzi, *Discorso naturale*, p. 23, remarks that "a squared irony" corrodes "even the residue of desperation of the poet-Pierrot" and reestablishes a "fundamental equalization between him and the world."

55. *L'opera in versi*, p. 11.

56. See Jarocinski, *Debussy*, p. 173.

57. *L'opera in versi*, p. 722. On this subject see the chapter "Le reazioni di Montale," in Annalisa Cima and Cesare Segre, eds., *Eugenio Montale* (Milan: Rizzoli, 1977), p. 196: questioned

whether he translated "bugle" with "suono di corno" instead of "buccina" or "fanfara" because the latter terms denote alarm (as Marisa Bulgheroni had suggested, ibid., pp. 98–99), Montale replied: "Perhaps 'suono di corno' sounded better for me than other possible synonyms; and among the many types of horns, I could have thought of the English horn: it produces a certain lament which would go well here. Anyway, often it happens that mistakes are felicitous."

58. *L'opera in versi*, p. 5. It is to be noted that the wind enters domineeringly the very first poems of the young Montale, as can be documented by these 1917 entries in his *Quaderno genovese*, pp. 14 and 50: "Il vento fischia / gli alberi si confondono in mischia" (The wind whistles / the trees are confused in a struggle) and "Impressione: Le sonagliere del vento squillano tra gli alberi primaverili" (Impression: The bells of the wind peal amidst the spring trees); beside the wind, "alberi" will be found again in "Corno inglese" and "sonagliere" in "Falsetto." On the theme-words of "In limine" see the comprehensive essay by Emerico Giachery, " 'In limine' e la metamorfosi dell'orto," in *Letture montaliane in occasione dell'80° compleanno del Poeta*, ed. Comune e Provincia di Genova (Genoa: Bozzi, 1977), pp. 17–38; on p. 27 there is an important reference to Luigi Rosiello, "Analisi statistica della funzione poetica nella poesia montaliana," in his *Struttura, uso e funzioni della lingua* (Florence: Vallecchi, 1965), pp. 115–47; the table with the first 100 theme-words in Montale (in which the wind is in thirty-second place) is on pp. 138–39.

59. See the anthropological interpretation (after Victor Turner) by Rebecca West, *Eugenio Montale, Poet on the Edge* (Cambridge, Mass.: Harvard University Press, 1981), and the deconstructive (Derridean) one by Stefano Agosti, *Cinque analisi: Il testo della poesia* (Milan: Feltrinelli, 1982), especially pp. 83–84. We should at least recall Victor Turner's *The Ritual Process* (Chicago: Aldine, 1969) and *Drama, Fields, and Metaphors* (Ithaca: Cornell University Press, 1974), both of which develop the classic Arnold Van Gennep, *Les rites de passage* (Paris: Nourry, 1909).

60. See Juri Lotman and Boris Uspensky, *Tipologia della cultura*, Italian trans. (Milan: Bompiani, 1975), pp. 145–81.

61. M. H. Abrams, "The Correspondent Breeze: A Romantic Metaphor," in the anthology he edited, *English Romantic Poets:*

*Modern Essays in Criticism* (London: Oxford University Press, 1975), pp. 37–54. This essay develops an idea Abrams had already proposed in *The Mirror and the Lamp: Romantic Theory and the Critical Tradition* (New York: Norton, 1958), p. 51.

62. Abrams, "The Correspondent Breeze," pp. 37–38, 48, and 51.

63. In relation to the problems of tradition on the one hand and of lyric narrativity (à la Browning) on the other, it is worth recalling the essay by Robert Langbaum, "Romanticism as a Modern Tradition," in his *The Poetry of Experience: The Dramatic Monologue in Modern Literary Tradition* (London: Chatto and Windus, 1957), in particular pp. 9–37.

64. Cf. the valuable essay by Oreste Macrì, "Esegesi al terzo libro di Montale," *Letteratura* 79–81 (Jan.–Jun. 1966), pp. 120–69. Note 8 (p. 123) on the link form-soul-sigh-fancy (from Dante and Petrarch to Wordsworth and Pound) can be a useful addition to Abrams's treatment of the romantic breeze.

65. *L'opera in versi*, p. 91.

66. Cf. an entry in *Quaderno genovese*, p. 33: "*Illumination*. The sun arrow of greenish light, a greyish sea that struggles on the muddy shore and trembles and shines in all its scales like a gigantic fish."

67. On the rhymes, guttural and dental alliterations, and "phonosymbolic" vowels of "Corno inglese" see also Glauco Cambon, *Eugenio Montale's Poetry: A Dream in Reason's Presence* (Princeton: Princeton University Press, 1982), p. 14. Cf. also the chapter on Montale's "upupa" (hoopoe) in Giorgio Orelli, *Accertamenti verbali* (Milan: Bompiani, 1978), as well as his *Accertamenti montaliani* (Bologna: Il Mulino, 1984), with his splendid analyses of the significant-signifying sounds of the Montalean texts he examines.

68. This line by Shelley is used by Abrams in "The Correspondent Breeze," p. 43. But in "Corno inglese" there is more than an echo from "Ode to the West Wind." See, for example, the movement of wind and clouds "even from the dim verge / Of the horizon to the zenith's height," a movement which becomes "The locks of the approaching storm" (lines 21–23); or "If even / I were as in my boyhood, and could be / The comrade of thy wanderings over heaven, / As then, when to outstrip thy skiey speed / Scarce seemed a vision" (lines 47–51): these lines seem fully accomplished in Montale's "vision" of "nuvole in viaggio, alti Eldo-

radi, chiari reami di lassù." Finally, I shall deal with another important connection between Shelley and Montale in chapter 3. On Montale's knowledge of the English romantic poet see Barile in Montale, *Quaderno genovese*, p. 131 n. 80.

69. Morton Bloomfield, "The Syncategorematic in Poetry: From Semantics to Syntactics," in his *Essays and Explorations: Studies in Ideas, Language, and Literature*, pp. 262–74 (Cambridge, Mass.: Harvard University Press, 1970), pp. 267 and 269–72.

70. Ettore Bonora, *La poesia di Montale* (Turin: Tirrenia, 1965), vol. 1, p. 88. Obviously I cannot agree with his evaluation of the parentheses as "soft-pedal moments" in the composition (p. 87).

71. Giusi Baldissone, *Il male di scrivere: L'inconscio e Montale* (Turin: Einaudi, 1977), p. 1 n. 1, p. 123.

72. Bloomfield, "The Syncategorematic in Poetry," pp. 273–74. Other typically syncategorematic means are repetition and deviation.

73. In dealing with this ending, Ramat, *Montale*, p. 22, erroneously speaks of "a nine-syllable line," but notes with subtlety that the splitting into two segments "almost signifies the congenital discord of this instrument."

74. Cf. the already quoted "Cerca una maglia rotta nella rete"; but Montale's questioning recurs throughout *Ossi di seppia* (one thinks of "Crisalide" and "Casa sul mare" especially), and all the way to the core of *Le occasioni*: "La casa dei doganieri": "Il varco è qui?"(The customs house: the opening is here?), in *L'opera in versi*, p. 161.

75. How intrinsically musical "Corno inglese" is can be gauged also in a comparison, which at first sight might seem secondary or even improbable, between the second line, "ricorda un forte scotere di lame" (it reminds of a strong shaking of plates), and a technical remark made by a contemporary musicologist: "The technique of building the piano . . . had developed so that the piano was no longer exactly the one used by Chopin and Liszt. The greater tension of the wires . . . had taken away the old sound of stricken wires and, we may add, had given it *a sound of shaken plates*. It is precisely here that Debussy develops a new conception not only of sound, but of music" (Rattalino, *Storia del pianoforte*, p. 271, italics mine).

## Chapter Two. Ut Figura Poesis

1. Luigi Magnani, *Il mio Morandi* (Turin: Einaudi, 1982), p. 48. When Magnani told Montale about Morandi's praise, the poet kept silent and then commented, "You know, in Italy there are at least seven poets who are better than I am; but among the painters I believe I am the first one"; questioned who those fateful seven poets were, he shook his head, "laughing softly," almost as if underscoring the paradox of his statement.

2. On this subject see Eugenio Montale, *L'opera in versi*, p. 414, and *Pastelli e disegni* (Milan: Scheiwiller, 1966). An issue of *L'Espresso-Colore* 12 (Feb. 1971) contains the "Satura" poems accompanied by beautiful reproductions of the poet's pictorial works and by Giovanni Giudici's comments, "Le occasioni dipinte," pp. 8, 12, and 16.

3. Cambon, *Eugenio Montale's Poetry*, p. 226. See also other two judgments by Montale that are pertinent in this context: "I am convinced that all the arts have a common basis. It is a mistake to separate them categorically, as if they were entirely independent from one another" (*Sulla poesia*, p. 597); and "My drawings have anticipated my sense of humor of the later writings" (ibid., p. 607). It is worth recalling that Corrado Govoni, a poet Montale admired, used to insert drawings as an integral part of some of his "visual poems" in *Rarefazioni* (Milan: Edizioni di "Poesia," 1915). Sketches and drawings are also in the manuscript of Paul Valéry's *La jeune Parque*, ed. O. Nadel (Paris: Club du meilleur livre, 1957).

4. Juri Lotman, "Primary and Secondary Communication-Modeling Systems," in Daniel Lucid, ed., *Soviet Semiotics* (Baltimore: The Johns Hopkins University Press, 1977), pp. 95–98; and Lotman and Uspensky, passim.

5. Without going back too far in time, suffice it to mention Diderot and Lessing, Baudelaire and Ruskin, Proust and Pater, Bataille and Yeats. To give only a few contemporary examples, one thinks of the pages by Paul Claudel on Dutch and Spanish painting (*L'oeil écoute*, pp. 9–48 and 58–88), and those by André Malraux on Goya in *Saturne* (Paris: Gallimard, 1950) and also on general issues in *Les voix du silence* (Paris: Gallimard, 1951). *Processo per eresia* and *La putina greca* by Neri Pozza (respectively Florence: Vallecchi, 1969, and Milan: Mondadori, 1972), are stupen-

dous, imaginary reconstructions of the golden period of Venetian painting; in a less explicit manner, in Virginia Woolf's *To the Lighthouse* (New York: Harper, 1927), the end of the writing of the text by the author coincides with the completion of a painting by the character Lily Briscoe.

6. Precisely because of its empiric approach, I am not using here an otherwise valuable book, rich with particular remarks: Marshall McLuhan and Harley Parker, *Through the Vanishing Point: Space in Poetry and Painting* (New York: Harper, 1968). Svetlana and Paul Alpers have warned against the dangers of oversimplification in the comparison between literature and visual art, in *"Ut Pictura Noesis?* Criticism in Literary Studies and Art History," *New Literary History* 3, no. 3 (Spring 1972), pp. 437–58.

7. Cesare Segre speaks of "a compresence of a linguistic reading of the literary text . . . and an assimilation of its content" which occurs sentence after sentence, in *Structures and Time: Narration, Poetry, Models* (Chicago: University of Chicago Press, 1979), p. 11. On the reading of visual texts see Jean Laude, "On the Analysis of Poems and Paintings," *New Literary History* 3, no. 3 (Spring 1972), pp. 480–81, and Michael Baxandall, "The Language of Art History," *New Literary History* 10, no. 3 (Spring 1979), p. 460.

8. Baxandall, "The Language of Art History," p. 461. Giorgio Patrizi gives an intriguing and brilliant account of many a specimen of Italian art criticism as dominated by a "narrative principle" which, far from resolving the conflict between the iconic and the discursive, continues the primacy of the written (rational) word over the image, the figural considered at best as "a secondary rationality," in "La 'lettura' dell'arte," in Giovanni Previtali and Federico Zeri, eds., *Storia dell'arte italiana* (Turin: Einaudi, 1981), part 3, vol. 3, *Conservazione Falso Restauro*, pp. 197–276, especially pp. 200–202.

9. Louis Marin, *Études sémiologiques: écritures, peintures* (Paris: Klincksieck, 1971), and Jean-François Lyotard, *Discourse, figure* (Paris: Klincksieck, 1971). All page references will be to these editions. Also Jean Louis Schefer's *Scénographie d'un tableau* (Paris: Seuil, 1971) should be considered in the same perspective from which I discuss Marin.

10. Louis Marin's analysis of "Et in Arcadia Ego" is in his *Détruire la peinture* (Paris: Galilée, 1977).

11. See also Jacques Derrida, *La vérité en peinture* (Paris: Flammarion, 1978), particularly "Restitution de la vérité en pointure" (pp. 285–305). Derrida starts from the polemic of the art critic Meyer Schapiro with Heidegger's *The Origin of Painting* on the "attribution" of two boots in a Van Gogh painting and proceeds to question such fundamental notions as matter, form, thing, product, and subject. A philosophical discussion of Lyotard (as well as Derrida and De Man) is in Rodolphe Gasché, "Deconstruction as Criticism," *Glyph* 6 (1979), pp. 177–215.

12. Wolfgang Iser, "The Current Situation of Literary Theory: Key Concepts and the Imaginary," *New Literary History* 11, no. 1 (Autumn 1979), p. 18.

13. Gilbert Durand, *Les structures anthropologiques de l'Imaginaire* (Paris: PUF, 1963). All page references will be to the Italian edition, *Le strutture antropologiche dell'immaginario* (Bari: Dedalo, 1972).

14. See E. H. Gombrich, *The Sense of Order: A Study in the Psychology of Decorative Art* (Ithaca: Cornell University Press, 1979), especially pp. 285–305, on the "sequentiality" of figurative reading and on the possible analogies between music and drawing (the tonal system is somehow analogous to perspective, while melody can be compared with realistic representation).

15. Rudolf Arnheim, "A Plea for Visual Thinking," *Critical Inquiry* 6, no. 3 (Spring 1980), pp. 489–97, which follows his *Visual Thinking* (Berkeley: University of California Press, 1969); Pierre Francastel, *Le figure et le lieu: l'ordre visuel du Quattrocento* (Paris: Gallimard, 1969), and *La sociologie de l'art et sa vocation interdisciplinaire: l'oeuvre et l'influence de Pierre Francastel* (Paris: Denoel/Gonthier, 1976).

16. W.J.T. Mitchell, "Spatial Form in Literature," *Critical Inquiry* 6, no. 3 (Spring 1980), pp. 541 and 560–61. The essay is reprinted, with the subtitle "Toward a General Theory," in the volume edited by Mitchell, *The Language of Images* (Chicago: University of Chicago Press, 1980), pp. 271–99.

17. Marc-Eli Blanchard, *Description: Sign, Self, Desire: Critical Theory in the Wake of Semiotics* (The Hague: Mouton, 1980), especially pp. 4–5 and 17–19. See also the recent overview by Wendy Steiner, *The Colors of Rhetoric: Problems in the Relation between Mod-*

*ern Literature and Painting* (Chicago: University of Chicago Press, 1982).

18. Juri Lotman, *The Structure of the Artistic Text* (Ann Arbor: University of Michigan Press, 1977), p. 217; more generally, Omar Calabrese, ed., *Semiotica della pittura* (Milan: Il Saggiatore, 1980).

19. On the importance of history in general see Segre, *Structures and Time*, passim; and in particular see Laude, "Analysis," p. 483: "Poetry and painting constitute series which, each one taken separately, are linked not to each other but to an identical sequence of a common cultural area. . . . To relate poetry to painting means, first of all, to restrict oneself to a historical area beyond which one risks posing problems only in an abstract way." Also Svetlana and Paul Alpers, "*Ut Pictura Noesis?*" p. 449, stress the point that the important differences are not among arts, but among cultural epochs.

20. On *La Voce* and *La Ronda* see Giorgio Luti, *Cronache letterarie tra le due guerre, 1920–1940* (Bari: Laterza, 1966), pp. 9–43; on the relationship between *La Ronda* and *Valori plastici* (or between classicism and traditionalism on the one hand, and metaphysical painting on the other), there are important remarks in Riccardo Scrivano, " 'La Ronda' e i rondisti," in *Letteratura italiana contemporanea* (Rome: Lucarini, 1980), pp. 41–82. Cf. also Paolo Fossati, *"Valori plastici" 1918–1922* (Turin: Einaudi, 1982).

21. For example, in Roberto Longhi there is a typical understatement: "Morandi will be considered second to no one," in *Da Cimabue a Morandi* (Milan: Mondadori, 1973), p. 1102. Giulio Carlo Argan defines Morandi as "undoubtedly the greatest Italian painter of this century" and "the only one that can be said to be truly European," in *L'arte moderna, 1770–1970* (Florence: Sansoni, 1970), p. 455. Roberto Longhi (1890–1970), one of the most influential art critics in Italy, knew and appreciated Morandi from the beginning. He taught at the universities of Rome, Bologna, and Florence. He founded the prestigious journal *Paragone*, devoted to both arts and literature, which was carried on after his death by his wife, the writer Anna Banti. Some of his works remain fundamental: *Piero della Francesca, Officina ferrarese, Il Caravaggio*, and *Viatico per cinque secoli di pittura veneziana*. A valuable anthology, edited by Gianfranco Contini, is appropriately titled *Da Cimabue a Morandi*.

22. Montale, *Sulla poesia*, p. 256.

23. Maurizio Calvesi, *La metafisica schiarita: Da De Chirico a Carrà, da Morandi a Savinio* (Milan: Feltrinelli, 1982), pp. 76–82.

24. On this subject see the analysis by Fausto Montanari, "Alla maniera di Filippo De Pisis nell'inviargli questo libro," in *Letture montaliane*, pp. 121–25, and Calvesi's pages on Carrà's "metaphysics" based on the "recovery of the object" and wholly distinct from De Chirico's (*La metafisica schiarita*, p. 216).

25. The most sympathetic witness of the *Anni con Giorgio Morandi*, Giuseppe Raimondi, is also the coeditor (with G. Bonsanti) of Vincenzo Cardarelli's *Opere complete* (Milan: Mondadori, 1962), as well as the author of the essay "La congiuntura metafisica Morandi-Carrà," in *Paragone* 2, no. 19 (1951). Sergio Solmi speaks of Cardarelli's "desperate classicism" in *Scrittori negli anni*, p. 207. The anastatic reprinting of *Il sole a picco* is now available (Bologna: Nuova Alfa, 1984), with a note by Stefano Calabrese, "Morandismo di Cardarelli."

26. Italo Calvino, "Main Currents in Italian Fiction Today," *Italian Quarterly* 4, no. 13–14 (Spring–Summer 1960), p. 6. It is interesting to note that in the Italian version, which appeared in *Una pietra sopra: Discorsi di letteratura e società* (Turin: Einaudi, 1980), Calvino adds Ungaretti to the previous selection (p. 49).

27. Francesco Arcangeli, *Giorgio Morandi* (Milan: Edizioni del Milione, 1968), p. 181. All page references will be to this edition. Francesco Arcangeli (1915–1974) was perhaps the most talented and certainly the most generous of Longhi's disciples, and succeeded him on the chair of history of art at the University of Bologna. He remains the best interpreter of Morandi (his 1968 monograph is a touchstone), and his essays on modern and contemporary painting, collected in two volumes under the title *Dal Romanticismo all'informale* (From Turner to Pollock) are equally stimulating and fascinating. A few of his pages are available in English as "Wiligelmus: Body and Nature in Romanesque Art," *Italian Quarterly* 16, no. 62–63 (Fall–Winter 1962), pp. 3–16.

28. See n. 3, chapter 1; see also Vittorio Strada, "Dialogo con Bachtin," *Intersezioni* 1, no. 1 (April 1980), pp. 115–24.

29. See Hans Robert Jauss, "Literary History as a Challenge to Literary Theory," *New Literary History* 2, no. 1 (Autumn 1970), pp. 7–37, and Rien T. Segers, "An Interview with Hans Robert Jauss," *New Literary History* 9, no. 1 (Autumn 1979), pp. 83–95.

30. It should be noted that I am not positing temporal limits for Morandi's works. The etchings I have chosen are mostly from 1912 to 1934; one is from 1942 and one from 1956, while all the *Ossi di seppia* poems are from 1916 to 1928. However, in cultural terms, both artists belong indisputably to the same "period," which may include temporal oscillations or notable delays between different art forms.

31. Marin, *Détruire la peinture*, pp. 92–93. On the origins of the still life as a genre see E. H. Gombrich, *Meditations on a Hobby-Horse* (London: Phaidon, 1978), pp. 95–105; on the interpretive problems specific to this genre see Marc-Eli Blanchard, "Natures mortes: Pour une théorie de la désignation en peinture," *Communications* 34 (1981), pp. 41–60, and Norman Bryson, "Chardin and the Text of Still Life," *Critical Inquiry* 15, no. 2 (Winter 1989), pp. 227–52.

32. Longhi, *Da Cimabue a Morandi*, p. 1098; see also Sergio Solmi, *Pittori di ieri e di oggi* (Milan: Ferrania, 1949), p. 92: the "accidental" of a natural impression is juxtaposed with "the absolute" of the stylistic definition; and Joan M. Lukach, "Giorgio Morandi, 20th Century Modern: Toward a Better Understanding of his Art, 1910 to 1943," in *Giorgio Morandi: An Exhibition Organized by the Des Moines Art Center*, pp. 19–39 (Exh. cat., Des Moines Art Center, 1981), pp. 35 and 37: "Pushing his objects to the point of abstraction, but never quite destroying them," Morandi used them "as compositional elements, . . . nearly as abstract and non-literary as the geometric forms in the works Kandinsky painted in the same years." Analogously Kenneth Baker, "Redemption Through Painting: Late Works of Morandi," ibid., pp. 41–45, writes on p. 42: "It was not these things that mattered to the artist, but their way of providing a pretext for representation."

33. Cf. Pier Giovanni Castagnoli, "L'occhio che accarezzava pareti vegetali," *La Repubblica*, Aug. 18, 1978, p. 19: "Toward the end of the twenties Morandi begins to besiege the form of things to the point of disfiguring it, and sinks it into the tragic clot of a desolate matter"; his art "continues to speak about painting but at the same time about a human condition of existence."

34. Francesco Arcangeli, *Dal Romanticismo all'informale* (Turin: Einaudi, 1977), p. 262.

35. Lamberto Vitali, *L'opera grafica di Giorgio Morandi* (Turin: Einaudi, 1980), p. 22.

36. Arcangeli, *Dal Romanticismo all'informale*, p. 270.

37. On the thematic aspects of Morandi's etchings see one of the very few essays on the subject, clearly written and persuasive: Amy Namowitz Worthen, "Giorgio Morandi as an Etcher," in *Giorgio Morandi: An Exhibition Organized by the Des Moines Art Center*, pp. 47–55, in particular pp. 47–50. On the "Bolognese tradition" of the network see Calvesi, *La metafisica schiarita*, p. 221. We should also remember the precedent of Rembrandt, who used to paint by employing the technique of etching: see Henri Focillon, *Vie des formes* (Paris: PUF, 1964).

38. Vitali, *L'opera grafica di Giorgio Morandi*, already quoted.

39. Cf. Durand, *Le strutture antropologiche*, part 2, chapter 3, pp. 269ff. Besides repetition-variation of a theme, the mystical structures of the imaginary include the "viscosity" of style (which tends to "glue" together disparate elements of experience), sensorial realism, and a tendency to miniaturize or "Gulliverize" representation. All have in common the emphasis on intimacy, typical of the "nocturnal regimen" of the imaginary.

40. Namowitz Worthen, "Giorgio Morandi as an Etcher," p. 51, italics mine.

41. Vitali, *L'opera grafica di Giorgio Morandi*, p. 21.

42. Namowitz Worthen, "Giorgio Morandi as an Etcher," p. 53.

43. Wallace Stevens, "The Relations Between Poetry and Painting," in *The Necessary Angel: Essays in Reality and Imagination* (New York: Vintage, 1951), p. 166.

44. Namowitz Worthen, "Giorgio Morandi as an Etcher," p. 53. It is interesting to note that other critics have also pointed out the distance in certain works by Morandi and their optical effect. For instance, for Robert Hughes the thin bottlenecks vaguely recall the towers of Bologna and San Gimignano ("Master of Unfussed Clarity," *Time*, Dec. 21, 1981, pp. 58–59); similarly, for Renato Barilli, "bottles, boxes, teapots, etc., become a wall in front of us, stand like buildings, walled towers, fortresses—thus he succeeds in organizing the surrounding territory with extreme precision" ("Un grattacielo in bottiglia," *L'Espresso*, Aug. 20, 1978, p. 55).

45. Vitali, *L'opera grafica di Giorgio Morandi*, p. 20.

46. Vitali, *L'opera grafica di Giorgio Morandi*, p. 16. See also his *Morandi: Catalogo generale* (Milan: Electa, 1977), p. 12: "The same, constant need to proceed by variations of few, exclusive, essential themes, which led the artist to become almost morbidly fond of some humble objects . . . explains as well his predilection for the landscape of Grizzana and its subdued, almost hidden beauty." See also his other important contribution, *Giorgio Morandi pittore* (Milan: Edizioni del Milione, 1965).

47. See Cesare Brandi, *Morandi lungo il cammino* (Milan: Rizzoli, 1970), p. 13. This book takes up his preceding *Giorgio Morandi* (Florence: Le Monnier, 1942 and 1953). See also Giuseppe Marchiori, *Arte e artisti d'avanguardia in Italia (1910–1950)* (Milan: Edizioni di Comunità, 1960), pp. 106–16.

48. Cf. Longhi, *Da Cimabue a Morandi*, p. 1096 (a "preferential list" by Morandi includes: "Giotto, Masaccio, Piero, Bellini, Titian, Chardin, Corot, Renoir, Cézanne"); and Argan, *L'arte moderna*, pp. 455 and 598–602: "Mondrian begins with empirical space, the environment, and arrives at a theoretical space; Morandi starts with a theoretical space and arrives at concrete space, the environmental unit. Paradoxically, in modern painting Mondrian is Paolo Uccello, Morandi is Vermeer"(p. 598). One is also tempted to attribute to Morandi some remarks by Claudel: in Dutch painting (especially in Vermeer) he sees "the image of thought which closes upon its possessions," and he considers light in Rembrandt as "the support and an emanation of thought" (*L'oeil écoute*, pp. 21 and 41).

49. Svetlana and Paul Alpers, *"Ut Pictura Noesis?"* p. 458, explain that the tone of voice implies the presence of a person who speaks, while no aspect of painting suggests the presence of a painter so decisively.

50. Francesco Arcangeli, " 'Tempo' indimenticabile," *Letteratura* 79–81 (Jan.–Jun. 1966), pp. 255–56. But in Morandi, too, the use of time, corresponding to the variations of natural light, is a "tacit theme"; see Baker, "Redemption Through Painting," pp. 43–44.

51. Montale, *L'opera in versi*, p. 9. All quotations from *Ossi di seppia* are from this edition.

52. See Pier Vincenzo Mengaldo, "Da D'Annunzio a Montale," in *Ricerche sulla lingua poetica contemporanea*, pp. 161–259 (Padua: Liviana, 1966), now in *La tradizione del Novecento* (Milan: Feltri-

nelli, 1975); Piero Bonfiglioli, "Pascoli, Gozzano, Montale e la poesia dell'oggetto," *Il Verri* 2, no. 4 (1958), pp. 34–54; and Arshi Pipa, *Montale and Dante* (Minneapolis: University of Minnesota Press, 1968).

53. Glauco Cambon, *Eugenio Montale* (New York: Columbia University Press, 1972), p. 7; "the etching-like quality of Montale's style" is briefly noted on p. 20. Mengaldo, too, speaks of Montale's "conquest of an inner, geometric, Morandian form of things" ("Da D'Annunzio a Montale," p. 252, in connection with Montale's "desperate rationalism" as well as the esprit de géometrie in contemporary poetry).

54. Gianfranco Contini, *Una lunga fedeltà* (Turin: Einaudi, 1974), p. 11. Born in 1912, Contini is an Italian critic who combines a rigorous philological preparation with an exquisite stylistic judgment and elegant writing of his own. Among the first to appreciate Montale's poetry, his "long fidelity" dates back to 1933. Perhaps his best-known and most valuable volume of literary criticism is *Varianti e altra linguistica*, in which his philological method of collating and systematically comparing all the different drafts and variations of a given text achieves refined critical results.

55. In a letter by Montale quoted in Alvaro Valentini, *Lettura di Montale: Ossi di seppia* (Rome: Bulzoni, 1971), p. 11.

56. Guido Almansi and Bruce Merry, *Eugenio Montale: The Private Language of Poetry* (Edinburgh: Edinburgh University Press, 1977), p. 32.

57. Giacomo Debenedetti, *Poesia italiana del Novecento* (Milan: Garzanti, 1974), pp. 27–40. Debenedetti (1901–1967) was a writer and chronicler who exerted a quiet influence on Italian criticism as a *critico militante* or free-lancer (see his three volumes of critical essays, *Saggi critici*, and at least *Il personaggio-uomo*). In the last years of his life he taught at the universities of Messina and Rome, and his lessons are now collected in such books as *Il romanzo del Novecento, Poesia del Novecento,* and *Verga e il naturalismo.* His broad European background and his interest in Jungian and Freudian psychology were models for generations of Italian students.

58. Almansi and Merry, *Eugenio Montale*, p. 32.

59. Ibid.

60. Nicolas J. Perella, *Midday in Italian Literature: Variations on*

*an Archetypal Theme* (Princeton: Princeton University Press, 1979), p. 242.

61. Durand, *Le strutture antropologiche*, p. 272 (Arnheim's "visual thinking" and Francastel's "figurative thinking" should also be kept in mind). Mengaldo, "Da D'Annunzio a Montale," p. 257, speaks of Montale's "rather closed repertoire of structures of the imaginary (metaphoric nuclei, images, and above all their contextual associations)"; these structures originate "a certain 'thematic monotony' and the constant reference to a numbered series of extralinguistic archetypes." Durand's categories provide just these extralinguistic archetypes and define them with precision.

62. The reference is obviously to Rebecca West, *Eugenio Montale: Poet on the Edge*.

63. Roman Jakobson, "Linguistics and Poetics," in Thomas Sebeok, ed., *Style in Language* (Cambridge, Mass.: MIT Press, 1960), p. 370; and Morton Bloomfield, "The Syncategorematic in Poetry."

64. Gérard Genette, "Métonymie chez Proust," in *Figures III*, pp. 41–63 (Paris: Seuil, 1972), p. 48.

65. Montale, *Sulla poesia*, p. 565; see also p. 88: "Eastern Liguria—the land where I spent part of my youth—has a meager, harsh, hallucinating beauty. Instinctively I tried a poetry that would adhere to every fiber of that land: and not without results, if a famed critic (Emilio Cecchi) immediately noticed that in my book [*Ossi di seppia*] everything happened as if under a veil of hallucination. Later on, in an imaginary interview, I tried to give a philosophical explanation of that fact."

## Chapter Three. Strategies of the Antihero

1. Montale, *Sulla poesia*, pp. 105–6.

2. Pier Vincenzo Mengaldo, ed., *Poeti italiani del Novecento* (Milan: Mondadori, 1978), pp. xxiii–xxiv and 527. The differences between the novel and lyric poetry are discussed by Cesare Segre, *Teatro e romanzo* (Turin: Einaudi, 1984), pp. 103–18, especially p. 115.

3. Romano Luperini, "Il 'significato' di 'Mediterraneo,'" *L'ombra d'Argo* 1, nos. 1–2 (1983), pp. 25 and 47.

4. Mikhail Bakhtin, "Epic and the Novel," in *The Dialogic Imag-*

*ination*, pp. 3–40, on p. 39; the following quotations are on pp. 35 and 25.

5. See *The Hero in Literature*, ed. Victor Brombert (Greenwich, Conn.: Fawcett Premier, 1969), pp. 11–21 and passim; and *Hero/ Anti-hero*, ed. R. B. Rollin (New York: McGraw-Hill, 1973).

6. Robert Torrance, *The Comic Hero* (Cambridge, Mass.: Harvard University Press, 1978); David Galloway, *The Absurd Hero in American Fiction* (Austin: University of Texas Press, 1970); Peter L. Hays, *The Limping Hero: Grotesques in Literature* (New York: New York University Press, 1971); and Bernard Schilling, *The Hero as Failure: Balzac and the Rubempré Cycle* (Chicago: University of Chicago Press, 1968).

7. Montale, *Auto da fé*, p. 168.

8. Luigi Pirandello, *L'umorismo*, in *Saggi, poesie, scritti vari*, ed. Manlio Lo Vecchio-Musti, pp.15–160 (Milan: Mondadori, 1960), pp. 158–60. On p. 130, *Tristram Shandy* is described as "a knot of variations and digressions."

9. In a review dated 1949, "Due artisti di ieri," Montale cites Chamisso as an example of the historical influence of a classic, *Sulla poesia*, p. 264; for another example, see his comments on Puccini and Gozzano quoted in chapter 1 in a different context.

10. Hannah Arendt, *The Jew as Pariah: Jewish Identity and Politics in the Modern Age*, ed. R. H. Feldman (New York: Grove Press, 1978).

11. Arendt, *The Jew as Pariah*, pp. 79–81; but see the whole chapter that gives the title to the book, pp. 67–90.

12. See Marina Beer, "Alcune note su Ettore Schmitz e i suoi nomi," in *Contributi sveviani*, with a preface by Riccardo Scrivano (Triest: Lint, 1979), pp. 11–30. Cf. also the well-known pages on Svevo's Jewishness by Giacomo Debenedetti in *Saggi critici, nuova serie* (Milan: Mondadori, 1955), pp. 89–94, and his more recent *Il romanzo del Novecento* (Milan: Garzanti, 1971), pp. 516–616 and 624. There are useful contributions in Giuseppe A. Camerino, "Il concetto d'inettitudine in Svevo e le sue implicazioni mitteleuropee ed ebraiche," *Lettere italiane* 25 (1973), pp. 190–213; Brian Moloney, "Svevo as a Jewish Writer," *Italian Studies* 28 (1973), pp. 52–65; and Enrico Ghidetti, *Italo Svevo: La coscienza di un borghese triestino* (Rome: Editori Riuniti, 1980), pp. 30–40.

13. Italo Svevo, *Confessions of Zeno*, tr. Beryl De Zoete (New York: Vintage, 1958), pp. 144–45.

14. Giacomo Debenedetti, *Il personaggio-uomo* (Milan: Il Saggiatore, 1970), pp. 70–71 and 36–37. We should recall that perhaps not by chance "inameno" (dreary) is the same adjective used by Longhi to describe Morandi's etched and painted landscapes, while "falotici" (extravagant) and "atona" (atonic) are typical of Montale's poetry.

15. Lionel Trilling, *Beyond Culture* (New York: Harcourt Brace Jovanovich, 1965), p. 64.

16. Debenedetti, *Il personaggo-uomo*, p. 81.

17. Svevo, *Confessions of Zeno*, p. 55. On the historical-literary models see Walter Reed, *Meditations on the Hero: A Study of the Romantic Hero in Nineteenth-Century Fiction* (New Haven: Yale University Press, 1974).

18. Morse Peckham, *The Triumph of Romanticism* (Columbia, S.C.: University of South Carolina Press, 1970). On alienation in general see Renato Poggioli, *The Theory of the Avant-Garde* (Cambridge, Mass.: Harvard University Press, 1968).

19. Karl Marx, *Capital*, ed. Friedrich Engels, tr. S. Moore and E. Aveling (Chicago: Encyclopedia Britannica, 1952). The critical literature on this topic is extremely broad. I shall limit myself to pointing out a few titles: George Steiner, *Language and Silence: Essays on Language, Literature, and the Inhuman* (New York: Atheneum, 1982), pp. 325–47 (among other things, Georg Lukàcs is defined "the true predecessor of Walter Benjamin," p. 331); Raymond Williams, *Marxism and Literature* (Oxford: Oxford University Press, 1977); and Gustavo Costa, "Vico and Marx: Notes on the History of the Concept of Alienation," in Giorgio Tagliacozzo, ed., *Vico and Marx: Affinities and Contrasts* (Atlantic Highlands, N.J.: Humanities Press, 1983), pp. 151–62.

20. Georg Simmel, *The Conflict in Modern Culture and Other Essays* (New York: Teachers College Press, 1968), in particular pp. 42–43, for the concepts of alienation and fetishism (from the 1911 essay "On the Concept and Tragedy of Culture") and pp. 47–67 ("A Chapter in the Philosophy of Value"). Cf. also a meaningful note by Bakhtin on this topic: "Literature is an inseparable part of the totality of culture and cannot be studied outside the total cultural context. It cannot be severed from the rest of culture and related directly (bypassing culture) to socio-economic or other factors. These factors influence culture as a whole, and only through it and in conjunction with it do they affect litera-

ture. The literary process is a part of the cultural process and cannot be torn away from it" ("From Notes Made in 1970–71," in *Speech Genres and Other Late Essays*, p. 140).

21. Cf. Simmel, *The Conflict in Modern Culture*, pp. 68–80 and particularly p. 77 on "naturalism" and "stylization"; and Wilhelm Worringer, *Abstraction and Empathy, A Contribution to the Psychology of Style*, tr. M. Bullock (New York: International Universities Press, 1953).

22. Joseph Frank, *The Widening Gyre: Crisis and Mastery in Modern Literature* (Bloomington: Indiana University Press, 1963): the importance of Worringer is discussed in particular on pp. 50–54, and it is from Worringer that the fundamental premises for "the spatial form" of modern literature are derived. W.J.T. Mitchell takes up and broadens this concept in "Spatial Form in Literature," pp. 539–67.

23. On this topic see Peter L. Berger, "Toward a Critique of Modernity" and "Toward a Sociological Understanding of Psychoanalysis" in his *Facing Up to Modernity* (New York: Basic Books, 1977), pp. 70–80 and 23–34 respectively; and Robert Dombroski, *Le totalità dell'artificio* (Padua: Liviana, 1978), pp. 138–43 and passim.

24. Berger, "Toward a Critique of Modernity," pp. 71–73.

25. David Caute, *The Illusion* (New York: Harper, 1971), p. 164.

26. Douglas C. Muecke, *The Compass of Irony* (London: Methuen, 1969), p. 215.

27. Ezio Raimondi, "Prefazione," p. x.

28. Paul De Man, "The Rhetoric of Temporality," in Charles Singleton, ed., *Interpretation: Theory and Practice* (Baltimore: The Johns Hopkins University Press, 1969), p. 198. It should be noted that in Baudelaire the term "folly" is always associated with the notion of "absolute comic."

29. Debenedetti, *Il romanzo del Novecento*, p. 419.

30. Eugenio Montale and Italo Svevo, *Lettere, con gli scritti di Montale su Svevo* (Bari: De Donato, 1966), p. 111.

31. In Italian the term "modernism" was originally used for a movement of religious renovation within the Catholic Church at the beginning of the century. Today the term has the same technical denotation as its English equivalent, referring to a precise movement in literature. See Robert Langbaum, *The Modern Spirit:*

*Essays in the Continuity of Nineteenth- and Twentieth-Century Literature* (New York: Oxford University Press, 1970); Frank Kermode, *The Classic: Literary Images of Permanence and Change* (New York: Viking, 1975); and, particularly important as far as an understanding of Montale is concerned, Hugh Kenner, *The Pound Era* (Berkeley: University of California Press, 1971) and *The Stoic Comedians: Flaubert, Joyce and Beckett* (Boston: Beacon Press, 1962).

32. Montale and Svevo, *Lettere*, p. 60. On p. 63 Montale replies: "I will make verse for some more years, because it is the only form I feel possible for me today. Do not be surprised that there can exist a temperament polarized in the sense of the lyric and of literary criticism: from Baudelaire to Eliot and Valéry, how many had the same destiny? And then, with the experience of life I have, wholly and exclusively inner, what could I say in the narrative field? I am a tree prematurely burnt by the sirocco wind, and everything I could give—halted cries and starts—is entirely in *Ossi di seppia*." Cf. Mario Martelli, *Il rovescio della poesia* (Milan: Longanesi, 1977), p. 47: "It is clear that between 1925 and 1926 Montale was reading Svevo with the same spirit with which he had composed *Ossi di seppia*." Similar positions are held by Gilberto Lonardi, *Il vecchio e il giovane* (Bologna: Zanichelli, 1980), pp. 1–32, and especially by Luperini, whose comments are worth quoting: "Montale translates his very modern discovery of a new human condition into the language of 'crepuscolare' tradition [for instance, the 'fanciullo invecchiato' of 'Mediterraneo']. 'Senility' for him is a trait of 'the newest Ulysses' and is to be interpreted in the context of a culture which sees in such 'senility' the sign of a disharmony with the real, of an unrendable laceration" ("Il 'significato' di 'Mediterraneo,' " pp. 35–36).

33. Cf. Angelo Guglielmi, *Il piacere della letteratura* (Milan: Feltrinelli, 1981), p. 17: "The fact that these three writers have dedicated the maximum of attention to problems of technique and language is not an indication of their lack of interest in reality; . . . on the contrary, it is the proof of their determination to establish a free and unconditioned rapport with reality—a rapport to be developed beyond the simple (and useless) objective of documentation and denunciation." An interesting statement by Montale should also be considered: "Pirandello? I know very well that he has turned European theatre upside down, and person-

ally I believe him to be better than Ionesco and Beckett" (in *Auto da fé*, p. 325).

34. Debenedetti, *Il romanzo del Novecento*, pp. 3–13. In such a context, he assigns a prominent position to Federigo Tozzi—and G. A. Borgese should be added as well.

35. Caute, *The Illusion*, p. 102.

36. Renato Barilli, *La linea Svevo-Pirandello* (Milan: Mursia, 1972), pp. 13–14 and passim.

37. Berger, "Toward a Critique of Modernity," pp. 70–78.

38. Renata Minerbi Treitel, "Zeno Cosini: The Meaning Behind the Name," *Italica* 8, no. 2 (Summer 1971), pp. 234–45.

39. Montale, in Montale and Svevo, *Lettere*, pp. 116–17.

40. See Wolfang Kayser, *The Grotesque in Art and Literature* (New York: Columbia University Press, 1981); Raimondi refers to Kayser in his comments on Baudelaire's "Essence du rire," when he explains that "since the grotesque has its end in itself, it produces a sort of new innocence, almost a joy that abolishes the dissonance of being degraded" ("Prefazione," p. xxv).

41. Italo Svevo, *Confessions of Zeno*, p. 11. Subsequent references will be to this edition.

42. Jacques Derrida, "La pharmacie de Platon," in *La dissémination* (Paris: Seuil, 1972), pp. 69–197.

43. Geno Pampaloni, "Italo Svevo," in *Storia della letteratura italiana*, ed. Emilio Cecchi and Natalino Sapegno (Milan: Garzanti, 1969), vol. 9, *Il Novecento*, pp. 493–532; on p. 523 Zeno's gratuitous act is "much more complex and I should say modern than Gide's," because it is "the objective condition of man in unreality"; Zeno "receives unmotivated responses from life."

44. Sandro Maxia, "Italo Svevo," in *La letteratura italiana: Storia e testi*, ed. Carlo Muscetta (Bari: Laterza, 1976), vol. 9, *Il Novecento*, pp. 505–55, on p. 548. It is interesting to note that Guido Fink linked Zeno's final page with Stanley Kubrick's *2001: A Space Odyssey* (and *Dr. Strangelove, or, How I Learned to Stop Worrying and Love the Bomb* should also be recalled in this context): "From the struggle of the apes with antelopes, panthers, and other primates there emerges man in a Darwinian process; from the double abolition of man and machine, perhaps, a new form of life, different and superior, will be born. If the monolith is black and shining, impenetrable, the Child has wide-open eyes; and he has undoubtedly the advantage of being free to roam at

will throughout a 'clean' universe which is free—but is it a consolation?—'from parasites and disease,' " "*2001*: Il cinema e lo spazio," *Paragone* 232 (June 1969), pp. 56–65, on p. 65.

45. Debenedetti, *Il personaggo-uomo*, p. 21.

46. Barilli, *La linea Svevo-Pirandello*, p. 12. But we should also recall Montale's words: "We had rarely seen a writer deprived of sermonizing and didascalic instincts," such as Svevo, who was "laborious and profound, entangled and extremely free, a writer of all times but a Triestine of his difficult years" (in Montale and Svevo, *Lettere*, pp. 93 and 174).

47. On this subject see Otto Rank, *The Double: A Psychoanalytic Study* (Chapel Hill: University of North Carolina Press, 1971) and *The Don Juan Legend* (Princeton: Princeton University Press, 1975).

48. Luigi Pirandello, *One, None, and a Hundred-thousand*, tr. S. Putnam (New York: Dutton, 1933). Subsequent references will be to this edition. The quotation from the original is from *Uno, nessuno e centomila*, in *Tutti i romanzi* (Milan: Mondadori, 1959), p. 1300.

49. Cf. Otto Weininger, *Sex and Character*, English trans. (New York: AMS Press, 1975), and Gaspare Giudice, *Pirandello* (Turin: UTET, 1963), p. 231. It should be noted that Weininger also outlined the "feminine" passivity of the Jewish anthropological type, and that Debenedetti took up such a notion and applied it to Svevo (in "Svevo and Schmitz," pp. 82–83). Cf. the well-balanced judgment by Ghidetti, *Italo Svevo*, pp. 35–36, concluded on p. 40 by a sentence addressed to Sergio Solmi by Svevo: "It is not race but life that makes one a Jew." Cf. also Alberto Cavaglion, *Otto Weininger in Italia* (Rome: Carucci, 1982).

50. Giovanni Macchia, *La caduta della luna* (Milan: Mondadori, 1973), pp. 265–66, but the first reference to Sterne is by Pirandello himself in "L'umorismo," p. 130.

51. Caute, *The Illusion*, p. 182. But he also adds, on p. 211, "Far from proposing that all the world is a stage, dialectical theatre insists that a stage is a stage attempting to say something about the world while remaining conscious of its own nature as a stage. . . . In these respects Pirandello's work is somewhat foreign to dialectical theatre."

52. I realize that the identity cards of these characters are extremely schematic: I have dealt with them more extensively in

*Literary Diseases: Theme and Metaphor in the Italian Novel* (Austin: University of Texas Press, 1975).

53. In *L'opera in versi*, pp. 82–83. The definition is Contini's in *Una lunga fedeltà*, p. 25.

54. It is important to note that C. F. Goffis, in concluding his fine reading of "Arsenio," emphasizes how Montale's "strongly intellectual capacity of analyzing the human condition" is wholly resolved in a "musicality" that, by "adhering to the existential moment," has become "an instrument for deepening knowledge," and by pervading the very structure of the composition has become its "soul and language," "Lettura di 'Arsenio'" in *Letture montaliane*, pp. 69–83, on pp. 76 and 81.

55. To this list one might add "stuoie" (as does Goffis, "Lettura di 'Arsenio,'" p. 74): "Every stanza begins with a hendecasyllable with accents on the second, sixth, tenth syllable and proparoxytone clause (*pòlvere, sèguilo, trèmulo, precìpita, stuòie*)." Besides emphasizing the technical precision of Montale's poetry, this remark is important because it shows the poem's deep musicality: what is dissonance at the lexical level becomes harmony at the metrical-rhythmic level.

56. Silvio Ramat likens Arsenio and Zeno as characters, and points out "the influence of the Svevian-Zenonan 'skepticism' . . . at this point of Montale's development" (in *Montale*, p. 67); Forti refutes this suggestion, and for his part proposes the name of J. Alfred Prufrock: in *Le proposte della poesia* (Milan: Mursia, 1971), p. 147 n. 16.

57. The similarity of the theme of contemplation and action in Svevo and Montale is briefly analyzed by Ettore Bonora, *La poesia di Montale*, vol. 1, p. 59. Cf. Teresa De Lauretis, *La sintassi del desiderio* (Ravenna, Longo, 1976), p. 150: Zeno's "sickness is nothing but desire, the abyss open inside the self, the *manque à l'être*, the motionless going of Montale's Arsenio"; cf. also Barilli, *La linea Svevo-Pirandello*, pp. 249–50: "Pirandello's 'exceptional moments' are perfectly homologous with Joyce's epiphanies, Proust's *madeleine*, and Montale's 'talismans.'"

58. Montale, *Sulla poesia*, p. 540.

59. Ibid., p. 124.

60. Ibid., p. 649. These words from 1951 seem to recall the "cambiare in inno l'elegia" (to change the elegy into a hymn) of "Riviere" (1920).

61. Cf. Gianni Pozzi, *La poesia italiana del Novecento* (Turin: Ei-

naudi, 1965), p. 167: Arsenio is "the dramatic figure of a character overwhelmed by his metaphysical incertitude as well as by the storm; he is the precise representation of an individual and at the same time emblematic existence; he is the conscious, although not peaceful, symbol of the existential anguish of an epoch, a generation, a human condition."

62. On this subject see Benjamin, "On Some Motifs in Baudelaire," in his *Illuminations*, with Hannah Arendt's valuable introduction, especially pp. 20–22.

63. It should be noted that Arsenio's solitude might be linked (analogously with Zeno and Moscarda) with a symbolic "absence of the father," at least inasmuch as "Arsenio" is placed in the context of *Ossi*: in the text of the poem, Arsenio appears "facing the sea," the same Mediterranean called "Padre" (father) in "Mediterraneo," the suite in which Montale describes himself directly, without an alter ego, as "uomo che tarda all'atto" (a man slow to act), and in which he also states: "E questa che in me cresce / è forse la rancura / che ogni figliuolo, mare, ha per il padre" (This, which is growing within me, is perhaps the rancor that each son, o sea, has for his father) and "dato mi fosse accordare / alle tue voci il mio balbo parlare" (I wish I could harmonize my faltering speech to your voices). Cf. Elio Gioanola, "Mediterraneo IV," in *Letture montaliane*, pp. 53–68, especially p. 67: "The paternal law generates Arsenio," for whom "salvation is not in a naturalistic dissolution, the extreme decadent alibi: it is only in the absolute Other."

64. Montale, "Italo Svevo nel centenario della nascita," in Montale-Svevo, *Lettere*, p. 169; Debenedetti, in *Il romanzo del Novecento*, p. 541, speaks of Zeno's "senseless moving which does not make for action."

65. I am using the verb "to resound" as John Hollander would use it in his *The Figure of Echo: A Mode of Allusion in Milton and After* (Berkeley: University of California Press, 1981); thus Montale is justly included, along with William Carlos Williams, Allen Tate, and Wallace Stevens, among the modern "echoes" of Shelley; cf. Abrams, "The Correspondent Breeze," pp. 44–45.

66. Stefano Jacomuzzi, *Sulla poesia di Montale* (Bologna: Cappelli, 1968), points out the derivation of Montale's words from Mallarmé: "les cendres, atomes des ses ancêtres ... Sur les cendres des astres, celles indivises de la famille, c'était le pauvre personnage" (*Igitur*, IV and V); and he suggested that such a "lit-

erary mediation, with the precise meaning it reveals (the ancestors, the dead), signals the accord between the final line and the 'iced multitude of the dead' which seems the end assigned to Arsenio" (pp. 102–3). Also, Marzio Pieri traces the "vita strozzata" (strangled life) back to an essay by Croce on Leopardi, in *Biografia della poesia*, pp. 186 and 224 n. 125. Such intertextual links as these are, of course, the very basis for a dialogic conception of culture.

67. Bernstein, *The Unanswered Question*, p. 318. On the preceding page he describes the three types of death Mahler "saw" in his symphony: his own, imminent death ("the opening bars . . . are an imitation of the arrhythmia of his failing heartbeat"), the death of tonality ("which for him meant the death of music itself"), and the death "of society, of our Faustian culture." In this cultural intertext which seems to multiply under the pen, it is worth recalling that Mahler was the model for that typical antihero in the guise of an artist, Gustav Aschenbach in Thomas Mann's *Death in Venice*.

68. Bonora, *La poesia di Montale*, p. 148.

69. Jonathan Culler, *The Pursuit of Signs: Semiotics, Literature, Deconstruction* (Ithaca: Cornell University Press, 1981), pp. 149 and 152.

70. Montale, *Sulla poesia*, p. 567. On this subject see Piero Bigongiari, "Arsenio più Simeone ovvero dall'orfismo al correlativo oggettivo" in *Letture montaliane*, pp. 421–39.

71. Caute, *The Illusion*, p. 261.

72. Ibid., pp. 261–63.

73. Frank Kermode, *The Sense of an Ending* (New York: Oxford University Press, 1967), p 98: "And of course we have it now, the sense of an ending. It has not diminished, and is as endemic to what we call modernism as apocalyptic utopianism is to political revolution."

74. Bakhtin, "Epic and the Novel," in *The Dialogic Imagination*, p. 38.

## Epilogue. The Plainclothes Clown

1. West, *Poet on the Edge*, p. 30. Her statement seems indicative of a broad critical consensus.

2. Raimondi, "Prefazione," p. xlix.

3. Eugenio Montale, *Fuori di casa* (Milan: Ricciardi, 1969), pp. 48–49.

4. Ibid., p. 49. The choice of the two non-British authors is not by chance: Montale translated Melville's *Billy Budd* into Italian, and his admiration for Foscolo is well known. I shall simply recall that for Montale, Foscolo belongs to the poetic school that "through the deepening of musical values tries to justify . . . those grey parts, the connecting tissue, the structural-rational cement which are rejected by 'pure' poets—if they are able to" (*Sulla poesia*, p. 112); and in "Intervista immaginaria" Montale also stated that Foscolo is "a poet who never repeats himself" (ibid., p. 563).

5. Montale, *Sulla poesia*, p. 570. Cf. also the sequel, important for the notion of dystopia: "The hypothesis of a future society better than the present one is not at all despicable, but it is an economic-political hypothesis which does not warrant inferences in the aesthetic order, unless it becomes a myth."

6. In Claire de C. L. Huffman, "Eugenio Montale: Questions, Answers, and Contexts," *Yearbook of Italian Studies*, 1973–75, p. 228.

7. Montale, *Sulla poesia*, pp. 569 and 562.

8. *L'opera in versi*, p. 278 (from *Satura*, 1970).

9. Ibid., p. 508 (from *Diario del '71 e del '72*).

10. Ibid., p. 1116.

11. Ibid., p. 535.

12. Montale, *Quaderno genovese*, p. 72.

13. Jean Starobinski, *Portrait de l'artiste en saltimbanque*, p. 10. All references will be to this edition.

14. P. 131. It is interesting to compare these remarks by Starobinski with analogous ones by Alberto Savinio of 1937: "Superior art is art as a passage to a superior world. It is an art that solves the problem of life, that provides a happy and immutable solution. Luigi Pirandello is one of these proud ferrymen. He is in the company of Picasso, Giorgio De Chirico, and Stravinsky," quoted in Leonardo Sciascia, *Cruciverba* (Turin: Einaudi, 1983), pp. 174–75.

15. Montale, *Sulla poesia*, p. 584 (1960). I find an indirect confirmation of my interpretation in Glauco Cambon's reading of "Carnevale di Gerti," the poem contemporary of "Arsenio" but inserted in *Le occasioni*. Cambon draws an interesting comparison

between the first part of the poem and *Otto e mezzo* by Federico Fellini (this other contemporary artist, also quoted by Starobinski, for whom the figure of the clown is fundamental): "Characters and symbols from the carnival or circus world finally come to the protagonist's rescue. They bring him back to the magic of childhood"; but "since the last strophic unit negates the spell," the end of the poem resembles *I vitelloni*, "a movie where the conclusive carnival scene seals hopeless disenchantment" (*Eugenio Montale's Poetry*, p. 35). These quotations confirm the ambiguity of the poetic voice and of the function of the clown in an extremely clear and independent manner.

16. Barile, in Montale, "Tre articoli ritrovati," p. 19; she also underscores that the young Montale, in reviewing Unamuno, appears to appreciate the latter's "continued leaning over the irrational."

17. Raimondi, "Prefazione," p. xiv.

18. Montale and Svevo, *Lettere*, p. 110. This sentence, dating back to 1926, was obviously referring to Svevo's Zeno.

# Index

Abrams, M. H., 26, 127n, 128n, 147n
"Accordi," 8, 15–18, 24
Adorno, Theodor, 122n, 125n
Agosti, Stefano, 127n
alienation, 79–81, 82, 86, 87, 93, 103, 105, 106, 108, 141n
Almansi, Guido, 138n
Alpers, Svetlana and Paul, 131n, 133n, 137n
*Altri versi*, 60, 84
"Anguilla, L'," 31
anomie, 80–81. *See also* alienation
antiheroism, 15, 56, 70, 72, 76–79, 82, 86, 91, 105–8, 113, 115, 117
Apollinaire, Guillaume, 122n
Arcangeli, Francesco, 45, 46, 47, 54, 57, 63, 68, 84, 109, 134n, 135n, 136n, 137n
Arendt, Hannah, 73, 74, 119n, 140n, 147n
Argan, Giulio Carlo, 133n, 137n
Arnheim, Rudolf, 41, 132n, 139n
"Arsenio," 16, 24, 33, 34, 82, 96–107, 108, 110, 115–17, 146n, 147n, 149n
"Arte povera, L'," 36

Baker, Kenneth, 135n, 137n
Bakhtin, Mikhail, 4, 12, 45, 70, 71, 72, 74, 78, 85, 118n, 139n, 141n, 148n
Baldissone, Giusi, 129n
Banti, Anna, 133n
Banville, Theodore de, 14, 19
Barile, Laura, 6, 18, 119n, 120n, 121n, 124n, 125n, 129n, 150n
Barilli, Renato, 85, 136n, 144n, 145n, 146n
Bastianelli, Giannotto, 6, 120n
Bataille, Georges, 130n
Baudelaire, Charles, 3, 14, 15, 24, 81, 82, 87, 103, 109, 117, 123n, 124n, 126n, 130n, 142n, 143n, 144n
Baxandall, Michael, 131n
Bazlen, Bobi, 83
Beckett, Samuel, 83, 144n
Beer, Marina, 140n
Bellini, Giovanni, 137n
Bellow, Saul, 76, 79
Benjamin, Walter, 5, 24, 48, 79, 87, 119n, 126n, 141n, 147n
Berger, Peter L., 85, 142n, 144n
Bernstein, Leonard, 8, 13, 39, 105, 120n, 123n, 125n, 148n

151

## Princeton Essays on the Arts

Guy Sircello, *A New Theory of Beauty* (1975)

Rab Hatfield, *Botticelli's Uffizi "Adoration": A Study in Pictorial Content* (1976)

Rensselaer W. Lee, *Names on Trees: Ariosto Into Art* (1976)

Alfred Brendel, *Musical Thoughts and Afterthoughts* (1977)

Robert Fagles, *I, Vincent: Poems from the Pictures of Van Gogh* (1978)

Jonathan Brown, *Images and Ideas in Seventeenth-Century Spanish Painting* (1978)

Walter Cahn, *Masterpieces: Chapters on the History of an Idea* (1979)

Roger Scruton, *The Aesthetics of Architecture* (1980)

Peter Kivy, *The Corded Shell: Reflections on Musical Expression* (1980)

James H. Rubin, *Realism and Social Vision in Courbet and Proudhon* (1981)

Mary Ann Caws, *The Eye in the Test: Essays on Perception, Mannerist to Modern* (1981)

Morris Eaves, *William Blake's Theory of Art* (1982)

E. Haverkamp-Begemann, *Rembrandt: The Nightwatch* (1982)

John V. Fleming, *From Bonaventure to Bellini: An Essay in Franciscan Exegesis* (1982)

Peter Kivy, *Sound and Semblance: Reflections on Musical Representation* (1984)

John N. King, *Tudor Royal Iconography: Literature and Art in an Age of Religious Crisis* (1989)

Gian-Paolo Biasin, *Montale, Debussy, and Modernism* (1989)